W9-CDD-194

Praise for *The True Nature of Tarot*

"*The True Nature of Tarot* encourages readers to learn and explore the art of tarot. Wing provides readers with insight into the world of tarot in easy to understand terms. She also encourages readers to see the good that tarot is. This book provides great teaching tools for the newcomer tarot reader and for those skilled in the art. There is so much great information in this book I recommend it to all people of all ages. After reading this book you will have a desire to practice the tarot! Thank you Diane."

Robin Marvel, author
Awakening Consciousness: A Woman's Guide

"One of my pet peeves is that tarot readers usually have no actual counseling experience and while they may be excellent readers, often the message doesn't come through clearly and/or cannot be heard by the client because of how the information is presented to them. Ms. Wing is well aware of this problem in the teaching of tarot and her goal is to provide tarot students with the necessary basic tools of counseling so that both the reader and the reading can be far more effective. Unfortunately, most of the tarot books I have read don't address this issue and this is only one of the reasons I think so highly of this book."

Ariel Monserrat, Editor/Publisher
Green Egg, a Journal of the Awakening Earth

"Anyone who practices, or wants to learn the tarot will enjoy reading *The True Nature of Tarot*. ...the little book that came with my old tarot deck, while it describes the cards and their meanings nicely, lacks what Diane's book offers; the permission and guidance to listen to your inner voice more as you perform a reading. Diane also speaks to the tarot reader from a professional standpoint. For those of you who offer readings to groups or individuals either for fun or as a business, Diane explains processes that help make the experience as pleasant and insightful as possible for both the reader and the seeker."

Nanci Arvizu, host of *Page Readers* on Blog Talk Radio

"*The True Nature of Tarot* is a useful tool for the experienced psychic reader or as an introduction to the curious and anyone who wishes to expand their understanding and use of Tarot cards as a tool for gaining insight. Diane's presentation is sensible, objective and easily accessible to novice and expert alike. I thoroughly enjoyed it and came away with an expanded view and understanding of the Tarot."

Loretta M. Vasso, M.S., CAC, CCP
Intuitive Counselor, Life Coach & Mentor and Tarot Practitioner

"Having had some incredible experience with Tarot card readings, I have been very interested in how the process works. The *True Nature of Tarot*, lays everything out for both the card reader and the person being read for. From beginning to end, Wing offers advice in how to prepare for the reading, do the reading, and gain insight into interpreting the cards. She also does an extensive review of the meaning of each card. From my experience, *The True Nature of Tarot* provides the most extensive, yet easy to understand review of the tarot card reading experience. I also feel that the author's explanation of how the cards should be used will help the reader gain understanding into how they can empower their lives by using the cards. Whether you are a novice or an experienced card reader, *The True Nature of Tarot* is a must read for people who have an interest in tarot cards."

Paige Lovitt, *Reader Views*

"In all the years I've been reading Tarot cards, I have never come across a book like yours!... I loved it!... It was very explicit down to the very smallest detail on each card... It made you feel very comfortable about the cards... Some books get too involved in the metaphysical and spiritual nature of the deck, but yours did not... I thoroughly enjoyed it from cover to cover... I teach the Tarot...I have been reading and doing ritual and spells with the cards for over 50 years Keep writing the way you do and more people will want to read more..."

Rev. Adele Basile of Mystikal Wonder

The True Nature of Tarot

of Tarot

Your path
to personal
empowerment

Diane Wing, M.A.

From the Modern Spirituality Series at

Marvelous Spirit Press

Library of Congress Cataloging-in-Publication Data

Wing, Diane, 1959-
    The true nature of tarot : your path to personal empowerment / by Diane Wing. -- [Rev. and expanded version].
        p. cm. -- (Modern spirituality series)
    Revision of: The nature of tarot.
    Includes bibliographical references (p.   ) and index.
    ISBN-13: 978-1-61599-021-4 (trade paper : alk. paper)
    ISBN-10: 1-61599-021-6 (trade paper : alk. paper)
    ISBN-13: 978-1-61599-022-1 (hardcover : alk. paper)
    ISBN-10: 1-61599-022-4 (hardcover : alk. paper)
    1. Tarot. I. Wing, Diane. 1959- Nature of tarot. II. Title.
    BF1879.T2W49 2010
    133.3'2424--dc22
                                                2009049888

Distributed by Ingram Book Group, Bertram Books, New Leaf Distributing

Published by Marvelous Spirit Press, an imprint of
Loving Healing Press
5145 Pontiac Trail
Ann Arbor, MI 48105

www.MarvelousSpirit.com
info@MarvelousSpirit.com
Toll free (USA/CAN) 888-761-6268
Fax 734-663-6861

This book is dedicated to my students.
You bring much to my life.

Contents

Table of Figures

Introduction

Since *The Nature of Tarot* was written and released in 2003, many have benefitted from the techniques and philosophy contained in that book. *The True Nature of Tarot* is a revised and expanded version of the first edition. In addition to the original text, it contains advanced techniques, card interpretations, and progressive insights into tarot as a tool of growth and enlightenment.

Throughout this book, as in the last, the same philosophy holds true: tarot is not a predictive tool, but rather a gateway to open us to the potential of who we are; show us the way to apply occult philosophy to manifest our desires; and to tap into the Universal Energy. With a strong connection to the Universal Energy, the individual is capable of creating an ideal present and future.

Tarot readers, beginner through advanced, and inquirers (those looking to experience a reading given by another or to perform a reading for themselves) will benefit from the information contained in this book. It is a boundless tool that allows the reader and the inquirer to tap into ancient wisdom that promotes deep transformation of the self and the way in which interactions with the physical, spiritual, emotional, and mental worlds are experienced. The mechanism by which it works is tied to the reader's and inquirer's ability to open to the messages and to relate to the energies that the cards represent.

Because free will prevails, no one can predict another's future. It is possible to convey the energies and circumstances that exist in the now in order to make changes that move one closer to desired goals; awareness of these energies does much to modify how a person approaches life. The decisions of the individual are what propel him or her to one future or another, not the predictions of a psychic.

The reader's role is to sense the situation and the energy of the individual in an objective way that allows the inquirer to gain a deeper understanding of vibrations that are not readily accessible to the average person. The noise of emotionality, stress, fear, and worry do much to cut off access to this information. The reader acts as a clear channel to allow the inquirer an unobstructed view into themselves and their circumstances.

Over the years, I have discovered and developed my own way of getting information from the cards. My techniques will be discussed throughout this text. While you are welcome to try my methods, I encourage you to discover your own unique way of reading and the meanings you attach to the cards. What works for one may not work for another.

If you have consulted a psychic or if you have done readings for others, you may have had encounters with the tarot that vary from mine. Results and abilities manifest differently from one individual to another. Through practice, it is possible to discover what your personal results and abilities are and the best ways to enhance them. The experiences of the reader, as well as that of the inquirer, are discussed throughout this text.

Almost a quarter century of experience with the cards has shown that the true nature of tarot speaks to the secrets held within its images. A tarot deck provides a pictorial journey of the self to foster connections with the Universal Energy and the Higher Self. The study of tarot and of the Self is life-long, with new discoveries waiting to be revealed at each level of development. The intention of this book is to open its readers to greater understanding and self-empowerment through making energetic connections that lead to wisdom about oneself and one's relationship with the Universal Energy.

1   The Truth About Tarot

Hollywood movies, fear of the occult, and the actions of unethical practitioners have created a negative connotation connected to the tarot. Some critics are under the false impression that all tarot readers are worshipping or representing the devil. Admittedly, it may be the case that some readers are practitioners of the black arts. For the most part, however, the opposite is generally the case. Psychic awareness is close to impossible without a belief in Universal Energy[1]. It is not the information itself that is evil, for it comes from a higher spiritual power; rather it is the intent of the practitioner that stains the knowledge.

A tarot deck is a tool that can be used in a variety of ways, just as any tool, knowledge set, or talent can be used for good or evil. For example, an incredibly brilliant computer programmer can create useful applications that benefit the world, or he can develop a computer virus that causes destruction and hardship for millions of people. Is computer programming evil? Hardly! It is the intention of the person applying the skill and knowledge that has the power to determine a positive or negative outcome.

In the same way, tarot can be used for the betterment of an individual or to increase their stress and worry, all at the sole discretion of the reader and the inquirer. The information itself is neutral, but subject to interpretation by the participants. The reader's delivery of information is critical in this regard; a message can be brought forth shrouded in darkness and dire warning, or it can be framed in the bright light of hope and positive change. Care should be taken when imparting sensitive information.

---

[1] Throughout this book, the term "Universal Energy" will be used as a generic title to refer to God, All That Is, Source, Spirit, Universe, and any other name that readers are comfortable with to represent this all-pervasive life force. Feel free to mentally substitute whichever name you are most comfortable with.

At the same time, the inquirer's reaction to the message is determined by the way the information is delivered and the emotional attachment to the subject matter. If you have avoided getting a reading due to fear of what may be revealed, remember that how the information is perceived is up to you. Many messages can have dual meanings, holding both positive and negative aspects within them. Information that contains elements that can be perceived as unfavorable can also hold valuable lessons. Messages containing detrimental components can also be taken as a warning, serving to help the inquirer avoid or prevent a problem. Within every circumstance, there is an opportunity for growth.

Keep in mind that in order for a psychic to read you, she must connect to your energy field. Open yourself to sense whether the reader is of the light or practicing in shadows. If the energy does not feel right, find another reader.

A tarot reading cuts through the drama of a situation and enables one to tune in to what's important. Issues will surface regarding personal and spiritual development. Much of what comes through reveals the inquirer's fears, hopes, and ambitions. It can be startling to reveal underlying causes for what is being manifested in one's life.

The information gained through a tarot reading should be used as a guide rather than a decision-maker. The tarot is a tool of enlightenment and understanding. Life decisions should be based on what is appropriate to one's growth, not on the prediction of a psychic.

Let's talk about how that information comes through...

Psychic Sensations

What it means to be psychic: A psychic is a person who has trained herself to tap into the Universal Energy and to open to the available information that lies within the energy field (also known as the *aura* or *auric* that surrounds all people and things. By perceiving this energy, the psychic has the ability to pick up information about the inquirer, as well as people and situations around her.

There are seven major energy points on the body, known as *chakras*, through which information can be perceived. When I read, the information flows in through the *crown chakra* at the top of the head, which is the center of divine connection allowing me to maximize the flow of energy received from the Universal Energy. Some readers pull energy into their *solar plexus*. It is important to be aware of where the energy enters and where it is released.

The ability to channel the energy during a reading is essential to the accuracy and the effect of the reading. It is also a factor of endurance (how many consecutive hours you are able to read before experiencing fatigue). To allow the information to flow in through the crown chakra takes much less effort than pulling information into the solar plexus. Creating a connection with the client through the solar plexus maximizes the connection between the inquirer and the reader, which serves to heighten the experience for both[2].

Opening to the energy: All people are born with psychic ability; yet, it is a skill that needs development. Some may refer to the potential to display psychic ability as intuition or a gut feeling. Most people have experienced knowing what someone will say next or that the phone will ring in a moment. It is up to the individual to open to the power available to all of us. Accessing this energy is possible when barriers and obstacles are removed, such as fear, jealousy, and self-doubt. These characteristics limit the ability to tap into The Universal Energy. Learning to move energy requires that the person be willing to open without feeling vulnerable. Most people have too much fear harbored within them to allow such an opening.

Getting a gut feeling and trusting it are very different. Differentiating between an intuitive message and a regular thought takes practice. It actually feels different. It's important to track the intuitive impressions you get. Generally, when that "little voice" comes through to provide guidance and you don't follow it, things don't go particularly well. I'm sure you've had this happen. On the other hand, if you follow the guidance, even if it's against all logic, things tend to work out for the best.

Jot down the times when you get a psychic impression and the outcome—whether it's for guidance or a premonition. In that way, you'll begin to feel the difference between a regular thought and your intuition. An intuitive message feels like knowing; it already

---

[2] *Reiki training is valuable to learn how to allow the flow of energy and to direct and transmit energy to and from various chakras.

feels true. A thought may feel more "filmy" and not so solid. Pay attention to those thoughts that "take you by surprise" so that you can use the information right away and begin to trust the accuracy of the message. Many people experience sudden glimmers of psychic awareness but are unable to bring it forth at will. Using a tool such as tarot increases consistency in pulling accurate information and provides a way to readily tap into your abilities. With practice using a tool, over time, you'll be able to pull information at will, many times without using the tool itself.

How information comes through: Psychic impressions come through in a variety of ways. Sometimes imagery occurs that is difficult to translate for the client. For example, I was reading a person who was asking about her potential for a serious romantic involvement. I saw a dog around the situation, but it didn't feel like a flesh-and-blood type of dog. I wasn't sure if the beau was a man who owned a pet shop, or had a dog, or just liked dogs, or what it could mean. A few weeks later, she met the man she ultimately married, while wearing her Scooby Doo™ T-shirt. It had been a cartoon dog that I was picking up on. I had been unable to wrap my mind around the exact nature of the dog and so was unsure of what it had to do with the subject's question. There have been many times when an image came through that was difficult to describe. This is what can happen when the psychic attempts to apply context to the impression. It has tainted some accurate readings in that the image was misinterpreted and incorrectly imparted to the client. Suspend personal framework and communicate the images you see without attempting to make sense of it. Many times, the client will know exactly what it is.

Personal feelings can really get in the way of providing an accurate, objective reading. An example of this occurred when a client asked me if his son's basketball team would win that evening. The five of cups came up, showing three spilled goblets of liquid and two goblets standing upright behind the person in the picture. I was not sure how to interpret this and the subject was putting pressure on me to prove my abilities. I felt that the son's team would lose, and felt bad having to tell him that. I was also concerned that I would put negative energy around the situation by voicing that prediction, thereby reducing the team's chances for winning. I was doubtful the team would win, yet optimistic that there could be a slight chance of winning in my response to the client. He took this as being unable to read the outcome. It turned out that the team lost by three points, hence the three spilled goblets.

Many times, what you are not feeling or not seeing in the cards is just as valid as other types of impressions that may come to you. To clarify what is coming through, be aware of what is missing around the client. A void or an absence of a person or energy within the reading can be very informative. For example, it might indicate that a particular person will no longer be a part of the inquirer's life. Also, share any emotions that may surface as you are reading the subject. It may provide clarification around how she perceives a situation or what another person in her life is feeling.

I have noticed that no matter what the subject's question is, the message will be similar with each hand that is pulled from the deck. It seems to come down to a central topic that the subject is overlooking or ignoring in her life. When the same cards are pulled repeatedly during the course of a reading, that is, in different hands the same cards appear, the message is trying to come through in a most insistent way. With 78 cards in the deck, the odds are against the repeated appearance of one or more cards. When a message comes through repeatedly, take special heed of that information.

For this reason, the overview in the beginning of the session, foregoing any specific question, give the Universe the opportunity to provide the message and then demonstrate it throughout the rest of the session in the context of the various questions posed by the inquirer.

Know the meanings of the cards in the deck, but look beyond the standardized interpretations and notice the details in the pictures on each card. There may be clues that will allow intuitive messages to surface. Say what comes to your mind even if it doesn't seem to make sense to you. If it is accurate, the client will know what it means.

Because what the psychic is seeing is not meant for her, but rather, for the client, the psychic will most likely forget what is said. There have been many times when former clients have asked me, "Do you remember when you told me...? Well, it came true." The fact is, I didn't remember, nor should I. Client confidentiality includes not mulling over information meant for someone else.

Types of Information: The type of information a psychic is able to access varies in accordance with her knowledge base. The information that comes through is reflective of the reader's scope of knowledge and level of understanding. The psychic picks up on information that she is familiar with. As growth and learning take place and the depth of understanding expands, there is a greater potential for profound insights when using the cards. As a result, it is essential to be self-aware and to expand your knowledge at every opportunity.

Generally, my readings focus on psychological and emotional issues that create blocks to progress. I can pick up factors that may be preventing the subject from moving forward or beyond a situation or set of beliefs. This coincides with my training in clinical psychology. As a result of my energy work, I am able to sense the energetic states of the client on both physical and spiritual levels and identify energy blockages.

Many clients want to know what the future holds. What is revealed is based on the person's current path. The ultimate outcome will be transient, given the nature of free will. The subject could leave my presence and then make one decision that could change the course of her destiny.

Blocking: I have been involved in private readings where it felt like the client had put up a wall and would not let me see past it. In one case, I was invited to do a private reading party at someone's home. One of the guests came into the room where I was set up. She sat down, handed me some money, and we began. With each statement I made, she emphatically denied the validity of what I was saying. We pulled another hand. The same information came through and her reaction was the same. Sitting with her arms folded across her chest, she informed me that I was totally wrong about everything. I could feel extreme resistance around her and knew that it would be a waste of energy to attempt to continue.

I handed back the money and told her that I couldn't take it as the reading did not help her or provide her with a valuable experience. I thanked her for the opportunity to read her and asked her to send up the next guest. Her jaw dropped. She reluctantly took back the money and quietly left the room. When the others had all been read, she came back, handed me the money, and asked if we could try again. She wanted me to keep the money, regardless of whether or not the reading was valid. This time, the subject seemed more open and more able to accept the message being imparted to her (it was the same message as the first time). She thanked me and left.

After the guests had gone home, the hostess told me that the woman shared what I had said with the group, and that I had correctly hit everything about the woman, but that the information was not what she wanted to hear. I thanked her for sharing that with me.

If the client is not open to receiving the messages she is meant to hear, do not force the reading or try to convince her of the value in the message. All that can be done is to ask the Universal Energy for information that is in the highest good of the client and those around her, create a relaxed atmosphere, and establish good rapport with the client. After that, it is up to her.

Validity: Validity has always been important to me as a reader. The client must feel that the reading is valid, but also, I want to be accurate. I want to be able to determine when the information is accurate and when it is not. When I'm on target, it feels different in the way it comes through. When impressions are muddy or feel slow in coming, I tend to question the accuracy of what I'm getting. It can also indicate how the client has been feeling and the way her thoughts have been flowing. I let the client know how the information feels as it comes through and, many times; the person will tell me that lately she has been feeling sluggish or foggy.

To keep the reading objective, I ask the subjects not to tell me anything about themselves or their situations. This is one way that I attempt to differentiate between what I know, what I surmise, and what I am psychically pulling in. Many times, I don't even ask what aspect of their lives they are questioning. Over the years, it has become apparent that when there is a message for a person, the cards portray the same answer no matter what the question is. I ask the client not to provide information or context during the reading, but to just confirm or deny what I tell them. In this way, I can avoid filling in the blanks with my own frame of reference.

When the reading is accurate, a sense of time is lost. I tend to speak more quickly and lose track of how long I've been reading the individual. I can see nothing else except the impressions that are coming through for the inquirer. It feels as though there is a pipeline of energy flowing between us. I am able to see interactions the client has experienced and to feel the emotions that she has gone through.

Psychic Peaks: A psychic peak is when you feel the most energized. It is a time during which the frequency of psychically obtained information is at its highest. Try to be aware of when your psychic cycles escalate.

At the beginning of my psychic development, mine occurred mostly in October. As I was born in early December, October is a time in my incubation that I was preparing to emerge. Each year, the scenario replayed, with my awareness increasing throughout the month of October. For me, autumn is a time of cosmic intensity.

Intuitive skills can be enhanced through Reiki exercises and grounding and centering techniques. In addition, using tarot as a tool evens out the peaks and allows my psychic abilities to flow more consistently. The cards help to move energy to pull information regardless of the season.

Adequate sleep, stress reduction, nutritious diet, and environment all contribute to the intensity and duration of a psychic peak.

Influencing Factors: There are many factors that can impact the energetic intensity and outcome of a reading. To maximize the power of the reading, it is important to test the variables that contribute to spiritual experiences and psychic ability. Many of these factors relate to the reader and the subject. These include the deck being used, the person being read, the belief system of the inquirer, the openness with which the inquirer approaches the reading, her level of fear regarding being read, the mood of the psychic, and the psychic's energy level at the time of the reading. Establishing trust and rapport between the reader and the client promotes a much more accurate reading.

Psychics have the ability to funnel energy in a certain way in order to pull information or to give energy to another. To maximize the amount of energy moving through the psychic, a clean auric field is needed. Healthy diet, attitude, and lifestyle contribute to keeping your auric field free of negativity. Drugs, alcohol (although I know some readers whose abilities are enhanced by a couple glasses of wine), and a poor diet contribute to a diminished capacity to pull information. As a reader, be careful of what you are putting into your body. Be especially cautious of animal flesh, as this tends to thicken energy, thereby reducing the flow of chi (energy) throughout your aura. This thickening diminishes the information that you are able to receive.

I have found that external factors can impact the ability to read. Any place that affords a quiet, energy-rich location is ideal for readings. It can be natural, as in an outdoor area, surrounded by trees, mountains, or water. Optimal environments for reading can be created, using incense, candles, crystals, positive images, and light-colored, natural fabrics. These elements do much to increase perception. Conversely, any place that is crowded with many people or surrounded by noise, clutter, and dirt diminishes the ability to pull information from the subject at hand. Elements having a negative impact on psychic openness include extreme heat, direct sunlight, concrete environments, and synthetic fabrics.

Large numbers of people concentrated in one area can create psychic distractions. At times, the energy of another person in the room may be stronger than that of the person you seek to read. This energy can conflict with the reading of your subject. An example of this comes from an experience I had doing readings at a corporate picnic.

The area they put me in was at a picnic table, somewhat away from the DJ and his speakers and the commotion that is inherent at an event of that type. I was in direct sunlight, which for me is not optimal (I prefer the shade, but it may be different for others). The line to see me was wrapped around one of the pavilions. A subject came and sat at the table and asked if her sister could sit and listen to the reading. I told her that it was up to her as, many times, information of a highly personal nature is revealed, and I would not want to compromise the confidentiality or integrity of the reading by holding back information so as not to allow another to hear. She assured me that it was all right, so I began the reading.

She kept insisting that nothing I was saying was correct. I told her that I was communicating the information that was coming through. Her sister jumped in and exclaimed that everything I was saying was describing her own situation! The sister's energy was much stronger than the original inquirer's, and so her information was what came through. At that point, I asked if I could be alone with the original subject so that I could attempt to read her directly. Smiling, the sister allowed a private reading, vowing to be the next subject so that I could finish telling her what was happening in her life.

When reading at major events, it is best to limit exposure to the blasts of energy that accompany large gatherings. Wearing black minimizes how much energy is coming through and helps to focus your energies and attention on the person at hand. It will help to filter out unwanted psychic impressions that only serve to confuse the message that is coming through for the inquirer. Black also serves to protect its wearer from negativity. When performing a private reading or healing, it is important to optimize the ability to open. For these types of sessions, I find that wearing natural fabrics in soothing shades ranging from white to green increases the amount of energy I am able to channel.

I have found that the longer I read in consecutive hours, the more awake I become. As the energy moves into my crown chakra and out of my mouth in the form of information, it has an energizing effect. I feel wide-awake and tingling, especially if my clients are open to receive the information. The exception occurs when the subjects are closed to hearing the intended message. Fatigue results, as this type of client has a draining effect on my energy. The opening that occurs during a psychic exchange leaves the reader vulnerable to the negative energy that emanates from some people, places, and objects. To minimize the effects of negative energy, grounding is recommended.

2   Grounding

Overview: Grounding is a means of attaching your energy to the Universe and to the Earth. By creating a connection, both above and below, a conduit is formed to allow a steady stream of energy to flow through you. In this way, positive energy flows in from the heavens and negativity flows into the ground. To attach to both is to know an intimate relationship with the Universal Energy, while experiencing an extraordinary relationship with the planet. It is not always necessary to ground in both directions. High-intensity situations require that you ground mainly to the earth; to do so stabilizes emotions and evens out extreme bursts of energy.

Grounding techniques are essential to a psychic in order to maintain a high energy level during readings and to avoid illness after the event. Before I learned to ground, I was reading at a large party. I was booked for the cocktail hour. The line was so long, that every hour for five hours, they asked if I could continue. The crowd was demanding and needy. By the end of the event, I was energetically depleted. I felt the effects of that psychic draining for several weeks afterward. I was wearing black at that event; yet, that alone was not enough to protect me, and I did not know how to ground and center at that time.

During a reading, there is the potential for the psychic to feel physical symptoms associated with the subject. For example, if the person tends to suffer from back pain, the reader may also experience pain of a similar nature in the same spot as the subject does. Grounding enables the psychic to avoid this type of pain transference.

In one case, I was reading someone and suddenly experienced a sharp pain in my head. When I told the client what I was feeling, she told me that she is prone to migraine headaches, with the pain being most intense in the spot that I was feeling it on my head. This has also occurred with back pain, sore throats, and panic attacks. One client had a severe anxiety disorder and as I read her, I began to have difficulty breathing and I felt extremely nervous. When I described the symptoms, she confirmed that this is what she goes through on a regular basis. Had I grounded prior to the session, this probably would not have affected me. It took 45 minutes, after she left, for me to fully recover.

Grounding Techniques

Instant Method

One method that allows instant grounding to the earth is to simply feel your feet on the floor. When we become upset, the energy rushes upwards, leaving the lower half of the body. In order to redistribute the energy, it is necessary to first realize that most of your energy has pushed itself upward, then to become aware of sensing the ground beneath your feet. Breathe deeply and feel yourself beginning to calm down. This method is also effective when feeling anxious or threatened. It allows the body's energy to root itself firmly in the ground and provides a stabilizing effect.

Personal Method

Being amongst trees is an important way for me to ground. In the forest, I can attach my auric field to the trees on either side of the path. That connection allows me to pull in fresh energy while dumping negative or stale energy into the earth through my feet. With each step, energy blocks are eliminated and replaced with the vital green energy of the trees. The woods encourage my chakras to open wider to accept the life force of the trees. The volume of positive energy flowing into me pushes away negativity and allows the light to flourish within me.

Not everyone feels the same strong attachment to the forest that I do. It is important that you find the environment that resonates with your vibratory pattern; for some, it may be the ocean; for others, the mountains may provide the ultimate sanctuary. You will know that you have found it when you experience a strong sense of comfort and openness.

Shamanic Method

Go outside and stand on a patch of ground (not concrete). Allow all the stress of the day, your worry, doubt, and fear to drain from your body, starting at the head and moving all the way down your arms, your torso, your legs, and out the bottoms of your feet. Let the negative energy flow into the ground (Mother Earth will cleanse it) until there is nothing left.

Move about ten feet from where you dumped the negativity and stand on a fresh patch of ground. Send your roots out from the bottoms of your feet into the core of the earth and pull up fresh energy, bright, orange light that flows up the roots and into your feet, up your legs, torso, arms, and into your head. Continue to allow this new energy to flow until you feel full.

Advanced Method

More elaborate grounding methods require at least 10 to 15 minutes to perform. Start by closing your eyes and imagining lines of energy emanating from your feet and moving downward through the floor, the ground, the layers of the earth, and into its core of molten light. Begin to pull the orange light up through the layers of the earth, the ground, the floor, and into the bottoms of your feet. Continue to pull the light up through your legs, into your torso, and up into your head. Feel the bright orange light filling your body and the strength that it brings. Take as much as you need. You are tapped into an unlimited resource when your energy string is plugged into the earth's center. When you feel filled to capacity, stop pulling the orange light, but do not disconnect from the earth. This will help you to maintain a firmly planted feeling as you move throughout the day. You are now grounded from below.

Next is to ground from above. Picture a large column of bright white light coming down from the heavens and pouring down around your entire body. Imagine being coated in this light from your head to your feet. Make the light solid around your body. Make sure all parts of you are covered. Now encase the white light with a thin, solid border of bright blue light. Beam the light out as far as you can. Focus on making it brighter and wider. Now your grounding and protection is complete.

With practice, you will be able to perform the advanced grounding method faster and more effectively. Try beaming the white light out farther each time, until you are able to touch objects several feet away on either side of you. If done correctly, you will feel energized, calm, and stable.

Now that you're grounded and open to receive messages, let's discuss some ways to pull the information from the cards.

3 How to Read the Tarot

Learning how to read the cards lends itself to discussions of both traditional card meanings, as well as non-traditional ways to pull information from them. Basic tarot card interpretations are provided in this section for your convenience. It is highly recommended that other texts are also consulted to get a broad scope of card interpretations from various authors. The book or pamphlet that comes with your tarot deck is a good source of information. From a non-traditional perspective, tarot can assist the reader in opening to another level where more information is available. The knowledge may come from the Higher Self, Universal Energy, the inquirer's auric field, or a combination of all three.

The more you know about tarot keys, symbolism, numerology, astrology, psychology, relationships, energy, and a vast array of general knowledge topics, the more apt you'll be to make intuitive associations and energetic connections during a reading. This will allow awareness of information that comes through with no association whatsoever to the customary meanings of the cards. This is the nature of intuitive tarot reading; creating an opening to a more expansive way of pulling information.

Various freeform spreads will be presented to assist the reader in making high-level connections not possible with some of the more traditional spreads that assign specific meanings to each position in the spread, such as the Celtic Cross. While this type of spread may be useful for some readers, I find that the information is restricted to the confines of the definitions of each position, and so prefer a more expansive approach.

Choosing A Tarot Deck

Tarot decks come in a wide variety of themes. A vast number of unique tarot decks have been created over the years. The body of knowledge that affects the development and use of various decks incorporates psychological, philosophical, metaphysical, artistic, and religious points of view.

To truly understand the scope of what is available, take a look at the four-volume set *Encyclopedia of Tarot*, an outstanding resource for those who wish to explore the subject in depth. Stuart Kaplan's work details the major theories of occultists and scholars. The text includes reproductions of cards from more than 1,000 different tarot decks.

With such a variety of decks available, it becomes your task to find a tarot deck that calls to you. Think about the types of things you are drawn to in everyday living. Do you gravitate toward mythical creatures? Try out *The Dragon Tarot* by Terry Donaldson. Are you drawn to a particular culture? *The Chinese Tarot* by Jui Guoliang may be for you. Do you prefer a deck rich in occult symbolism? Check out the *Rider Waite* or *Universal Waite* decks. Are you more comfortable with traditional tarot images that are colorful and simplified? *The Gilded Tarot* by Ciro Marchetti and Barbara Moore may be a good choice for you.

Look for a deck that vibrates with your belief system. Feel the density of the energy around the deck and scan it for vibratory impressions that may be aligned or in opposition to your nature. The more synchronized your energy is with the energy of the deck, the greater the amount of information you can pull from the cards.

The vibration of the deck itself can influence the type of information that can be pulled from it. For example, I use the *Enchanted Tarot* by Amy Zerner and Monte Farber for relationship readings, *The Mythic Tarot* by Juliet Sharman-Burke and Liz Greene for health readings, the *Voyager Tarot* by James Wanless, Ph.D. for blocks to progress and life path readings, and the *Universal Waite* by Pamela Colman Smith and Mary Hanson-Roberts for general information. The type of information available from a deck can also vary by individual practitioner. You may get a whole different set of information than I do from the tarot decks noted above.

In addition, the deck you start out with may not always work for you. The deck should be changed to accommodate any energy shifts that may occur within you. One of the signs that you have had a shift is when the deck no longer works for you. It seems as though the energy around the deck has died. You are no longer able to pull information from it. What has happened is that your vibratory pattern has changed and is no longer in rhythm with the vibrations of the deck. Expect this to happen periodically during your psychic development. Expect your psychic development to last your entire lifetime.

Before the Reading Begins

Knowing that the energy associated with the deck can vary, there is no limit to the number of decks you can use. I usually have between two and six decks that I am feeling connected to with me when I do professional readings and offer clients their choice of the deck they feel most drawn to. It increases the potential to create an optimum reading situation. Having input from both the reader and the client promotes a higher likelihood that accurate information will result.

There are psychics who prefer to use only one deck and do not allow their deck to be handled by their clients. By restricting the energies that are applied to the cards, they insure that the vibrations on the cards are theirs alone. For some, this allows for the optimum reading that they can provide. I, however, am of the belief that the investment of the client's energy adds a necessary dimension to the reading. In this way, a partnership is established, thereby creating an energetic link between the reader and the inquirer.

Trust is also a critical component of an enhanced reading experience; the reader trusting the messages that are coming through and the inquirer trusting the reader to work in her best interest during the session. Giving a stranger access to your energy field is to open your deepest thoughts and feelings for examination. This can arouse a sense of vulnerability that may inhibit the flow of information during the session. Trust should be established between the reader and the subject; an understanding that what occurs in a private session remains confidential. If there is no trust, the reading should not take place.

Setting up the reading

Shuffle: To begin the reading, the inquirer selects one of the decks that have been placed in front of her. Ask the client to think about things she wants to know while she shuffles the deck. This will infuse the cards with her energy and allow the client to focus on what is important to her. I recommend having the inquirer touch the cards as much as possible as opposed to cutting them into two piles, one in each hand, and fanning them together. The more the cards are touched, the more energy is transferred onto them.

When the client decides that the cards are adequately shuffled, she puts them in one pile face down. I wave my right hand over the cards to see if I can feel heat. If so, this indicates that the subject has put an adequate amount of her energy onto the cards and the reading may begin. If not, she continues to shuffle until her vibrations have been imprinted on the cards. The intensity of the heat indicates the extent to which the person is open to be read, as well as her overall energy level. The more energy on the cards, the warmer they will feel, and the more personal information will be available to be read. The reader may have alternate ways of determining a sufficient level of energy on the cards, and these should be used in place of the heat-sensing method.

Choose: The cards are then fanned out across the table face down in front of the inquirer. The number of cards selected depends on the focus of the reading. When the inquirer seeks information pertaining to her personally, she is instructed to select one card for each letter in her first and middle names and to put them in one pile face down. Let's say the subject's name is Barbara Ann. Having the subject choose cards in relation to the name on her birth certificate intensifies the focus on her particular vibration. Cards representing letters in the last name are not chosen, as the surname carries with it the vibrations of the inquirer's ancestors. If the desired information has to do with someone else, cards representing the name of the other person would be pulled.

When the question pertains to work, the inquirer can increase the career vibration by making her selections with her right hand. The right hand connects to the left hemisphere of the brain, where logic and structure reside. If the question is regarding more personal, creative, or romantic aspects of a situation, then it is best to choose cards with the left hand. The left is connected to the brain's right hemisphere where creative thinking and emotional response are predominant.

Take note of the way the question is asked when the cards are being chosen. It is best to frame the question that begins with "give me a message about…" in order to keep the energy open for an insightful message to come through. When the question is asked as "will something happen or won't it," then the energy around it is limited and will not provide the same level of enlightenment as an open-ended question will.

Layout: Picking up the chosen cards, turn them face up one at a time, placing them from left to right across the table. A new row is begun when it intuitively feels right to do so. The cards are placed with their corners touching. In this way, connections and relationships are established between the aspects of the cards.

A sample hand may look like this:

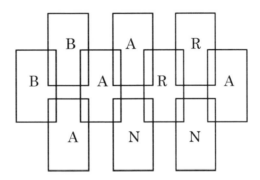

Example 1: Free-Form Spread

This is one method of laying out the cards, ideal for a general reading or the initial overview. There are many spreads to choose from, each with its own method and purpose, which will be detailed in the next section.

Beginning the reading: All of the cards are read upright. Some readers prefer to impart a reversed or negative meaning to a card that is upside-down when it is turned over. This method takes into consideration the interrelationship of the cards that are around one card or another to determine its meaning, rather than the direction it is facing, allowing interconnections to surface.

Once the hand is dealt, visually scan the cards to see if one draws your attention or seems brighter than the others. When a card stands out from the rest, it may look more intense or prominent than the others. This card may provide a starting point for the reading or indicate a primary issue facing the client. If the card feels especially insistent, it can indicate an issue that is occurring in the present and having a strong effect on the inquirer. Looking at the cards connected to it can put the issue into context of other circumstances surrounding the inquirer.

To clarify what is seen in the cards, notice the patterns and direction of energy that flows through the cards. Take notice of which cards are connected diagonally to each other. What connections arise? Does one grouping of cards seem to have a separate energy pattern from another grouping? Check to see if the energy is flowing horizontally from right to left, or vertically up or down. This gives an indication of which direction the cards should be read. Dismiss the way a book is read from right to left. Follow the patterns that are unique to each hand.

As various images and bits of information come to you, look at the card where they are originating, and then look at the cards around it. Begin to tell a story, making connections and putting together the bits of insight into a cohesive picture of what is happening around the inquirer.

As the messages begin to be revealed, ask the client to only confirm or deny the information that is coming through. It is best to know as little about the situation as possible until available information has been pulled from the cards. This allows the reader to provide the information in the most objective way possible. Knowing too much about a situation may corrupt the images that are coming through. The client is welcome to share the details upon completion of the reading. It helps evaluate the accuracy of the message by knowing the actual circumstances involved.

The first hand usually provides an overview of the most pertinent issues in the life of the inquirer. No specific question is asked for the first set of cards. Allow the Universe to have its say at the beginning to convey the message the client needs to hear, and then the client can have the opportunity to ask specific questions.

4　Seeing Patterns in the Cards

Spreads: There are many layouts in existence for use with tarot cards. Most are structured so that each position represents a particular aspect of the answer. The spreads offered in this section provide a loose framework within which the reader is free to make intuitive connections and reveal significant interrelationships between the cards without restriction. Determine the question before deciding which spread is most appropriate to use.

Free Form Spread: there are several types of standard spreads that can be used to deal the cards. For me, using a structured type of spread limits the way the cards can be interpreted. Spreads such as the Celtic Cross have strictly defined positions for the cards. Each position in the spread denotes a particular aspect of the reading, such as past, present, future, etc.

A free-form spread, such as shown in Example 1, laid out in accordance with how the energy is flowing, expands the type of information that can be discerned. If the reading pertains to the inquirer directly, ask her to pull one card for each letter in her first and middle names. If the reading is to uncover information about someone else, have the inquirer pull that person's first and middle names. Many times, clients are interested in finding out about their parents' health, their children's state of being, or their significant other's mindset about a particular issue.

With each hand that is drawn, a new energy accompanies the cards. There is a pattern and direction in the energy that flows through the cards. Special relationships can be seen in cards that are connected diagonally to each other.

Sometimes, one grouping of cards seems to have a separate energy pattern from another grouping. The energy may be flowing horizontally from right to left, or vertically up or down. This gives an indication of which direction the cards should be read. Follow the patterns that are unique to each hand.

The energy patterns of the hand can be used to reveal the state of the inquirer. For example, if there is the absence of a continuous flow, and the energy feels choppy instead, it would indicate that the person being read is feeling especially scattered; or that so much is going on that the person's life seems fragmented.

If the cards seem to energetically divide themselves into vertical half-sections (see Example 2), it indicates that the inquirer has two distinct aspects of his life that are taking priority over others. Determine if the halves represent work and home, or possibly two separate people who interact with and have impact on the inquirer. Note if there is a card upon which all other cards seem to pivot. This will reveal the crux of the issue that the inquirer is facing.

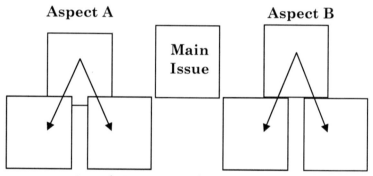

Example 2: Vertical Half-Section Spread

Quick Answer Spread: There are times when the inquirer asks a closed question, that is, one that can be answered with a yes/no response. In this case, the reader needs to provide the energies surrounding the question and communicate the factors that will impact the outcome. For this, the quick answer spread is a good choice.

The inquirer shuffles the cards while thinking of the question, and then cuts the cards into three piles. The reader turns over the top cards on each pile. Depending on the cards that are revealed, more information may be needed. The additional cut is optional. If so, ask the inquirer to cut each pile once more, putting each additional cut above or below the original pile. In this way, connections can be determined between the original pile and the secondary pile for each card (see Example 3).

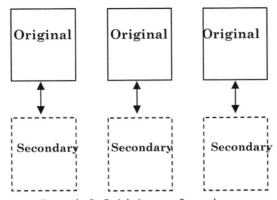

Example 3: Quick Answer Spread

Past Life Reading: the three card spread can also be used to perform a past life reading. The inquirer chooses three cards from anywhere in the deck, while focusing on the desire for information about the last life of the person that most impacts on this life. Clarifying cards can be drawn as needed.

Main Issue Spread: this spread works well in cases where the inquirer asks a question, where it is important, to find out the core issue plus the contributing factors. The inquirer shuffles the cards while thinking of the question. The cards are fanned out and she pulls five cards from anywhere in the deck, putting them in one pile face down. The reader picks up the cards and places them face up, starting in the left-hand corner, then the right-hand corner, the third card in the center, and then the remaining two at the bottom left- and right-hand corners of the center card, in that order (see Example 4).

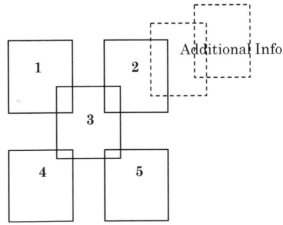

Example 4: Main Issue Spread

The center card represents the main issue impacting the question and the corner cards denote the variables that affect the main issue. Notice the interactions between the corner cards and the center card. If more information is required on a particular variable (corner card), ask the inquirer to pull two more cards from anywhere in the deck. Place the cards adjacent to the card which represents the variable in question. This can be done for one or all of the variables in the spread.

The Self: An alternative use of the five-card layout[3] is effective for understanding energies around various opportunities the inquirer may be considering. Use the same method of pulling the cards, concentrating on each separate possibility as each card is drawn. Name the card in the center "Self," (card 3 in Example 4) and look to that card to see what may be propelling the person forward or holding them back. Each corner card represents one of the opportunities she is considering; use these to get information about the possibilities around each. As with the "Main Issue" spread, pull two cards for each option that needs further clarification.

The Journey Spread: The Journey spread is valuable when seeking insights into questions about one's life journey, such as "Am I on the right path?"; "Should I be changing directions?"; "What should I be aware of as I seek to make appropriate decisions?"; "How do I remove obstacles and move forward?" It is ideal to use for journaling and to understand where you are on your path.

Begin by shuffling the cards and thinking about your life and what you want it to look like, the type of work you want to do, the kind of people you want around you, etc. Fan out the cards and choose seven from anywhere in the deck. Place the first five face up side by side across the center of the layout (designated as A in Example 5). The remaining two cards are placed above and below the center card (designated as B in Example 5).

---

[3] The alternate method of the 5-card spread was developed by a highly insightful student of mine, Aimee Kovac. She also designed the Journey spread detailed in this section. These are used with Aimee's permission. I am so proud of her for taking to heart the idea of assimilating the information I shared with her and going beyond it to create her own methods of reading that reflect her personal style. I encourage everyone reading this text to do the same and in that way, use the cards as a tool of self-discovery.

The first two cards in the row represent the first leg of the journey; the three cards comprising the center column designate issues and energies that arise at the crossroads of your journey; and the last two cards reflect what is coming up or the potential result after the issue at the crossroads is resolved.

Now, four clarifying cards are pulled from the remaining cards in the deck. These are placed above and below the second and fourth cards in the main row (designated as C in Example 5). As you look at how these four cards relate to the others, open to what new insights can be gained about the main path of the journey.

Finally, the last four cards are drawn and placed diagonally at the corners of the entire spread (designated as D in Example 5). These represent the connecting or bridging energies between the path itself and the clarifying variables. Again look with a fresh perspective to glean additional insights that are available through the addition of these bridging cards.

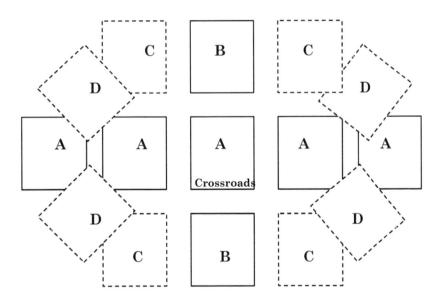

Example 5: The Journey Spread

*

5   Interpreting the Cards

Tarot lends itself to lifelong study, providing boundless opportunities to go deep into ancient wisdom. The symbolism, colors, Hebrew letters, biblical history, cultural interpretations, artistic interpretations, metaphysical and psychological concepts, and life lessons contained therein offer the serious student many avenues of learning to pursue. The totality of possible explanations is voluminous.

The meanings of the cards written here offer the meanings that have consistently come forward to me during years of tarot reading. I encourage you to consider these and about each card; meditate on each card and see what comes through from your personal perspective. Discover what it means to you, based on your level of understanding and experience. Over time, your interpretations will change and expand, becoming a reflection of your personal and spiritual growth and esoteric knowledge.

The following guidance and interpretations offered in this text are meant to provide a basic understanding intended to be used as a springboard for individual interpretation and further study.

Deck Overview

There are 78 cards in a standard tarot deck, comprised of the Major Arcana (22 cards numbered 0-21) and Minor Arcana (suit and court cards). Arcana are the plural of *arcanum*, meaning a deep secret or mystery. Generally, tarot decks include a book or insert that details the meanings of each card. It is recommended that the accompanying literature is read, especially with the more obscure or artistic decks.

The Major Arcana reflects big-picture concepts. At the same time, it takes us on a journey of self-discovery through the revealing of deep metaphysical concepts designed to foster a connection with the Universal Energy and with our higher selves. The sequence of cards 0 through 21 assists us in exploring our journey through life. Each Major Arcana card can be used as a tool for meditation. Take one card at a time and meditate on its meaning, symbolism, what it means to you, and how this information can be used in daily life.

The Minor Arcana reflects the details of what is going on and fills in the gaps between the concepts of the Major Arcana cards. They give a general sense of the energy around the inquirer and the situation. It is made up of four suits—Wands, Swords, Cups, and Pentacles—each representing a tool of the Magician. While each card has a specific suit designation, many times, more than one tool is depicted on the card. This signifies the need to use all the aspects of our power as humans, including the physical, emotional, mental, and spiritual gifts to tap into the Universal Energy and manifest our desires.

Each suit has associated attributes and elemental correspondences that provide clues as to the message of the card.

Suit	Aliases	Element	Explanation
Wands	Rods, Staffs	Fire	The will, masculine principle, creative energy, skills, work, development, initiative, progress, and enterprise
Swords	Daggers	Air	Conflict, cruelty, pain, and suffering. Indicates misfortune, injury, or some type of mental anguish.
Cups	Chalices	Water	Corresponds to the feminine principle, love, marriage, emotions, sensitivity, and pleasure.
Pentacles	Discs, Coins	Earth	Relates to material concerns: money, prosperity, status, and security. Can also indicate spiritual ties or motivations.

Associated Attributes & Elemental Correspondences of Suits

The Minor Arcana also depicts people who impact the inquirer by way of the Court cards, which include King, Queen, Knight, and Page. There may be slight variations depending on the deck; for example, the Page may be called Princess. In general, the Court cards represent actual people involved in the situation; however, there are times when they may indicate a concept or energy that should be considered in the scope of the reading. Try to sense if the card represents a person or a concept.

When the card represents a person, use the following guidelines to be able to describe the individual age. This can represent the person's physical or emotional age. For example, if the individual is a 25-year-old male but acts like he is 15 years old, then he may come up as a Page rather than as a Knight.

King is a man over age 35
Queen is a woman over age 21
Knight is a man aged 21-34
Page is a boy or a girl under age 21

Additionally, depending on the suit of the Court card, other personality and physical attributes are prevalent:

Suit	Characteristics
Wands	People with light or dark brown hair, light olive skin, brown, green, or hazel eyes, and/or a fiery personality
Swords	People with dark brown or black hair; fair or light skin; dark brown or black eyes, and/or a decisive, opinionated personality.
Cups	People with blond, light brown, or gray hair; fair to medium skin; blue or gray eyes; and/or a sensitive personality.
Pentacles	People with red, light blonde, or gray hair; dark skin; green or brown eyes; and/or an earthy personality or an understanding nature.

Personality and Physical Attributes by Suit

Now that we have a framework, let's do a deeper dive into the meaning of each card...

6   The Major Arcana

0 - The Fool

Key Words: Innocence, Optimism, Courage, New Potential

The Fool, designated as zero, the holding place for all other numbers, the beginning, the starting point on the journey of life.

Every time we are born, we begin our path anew and return many times until we have fulfilled our karmic obligations and learned required lessons. There is a certain innocence that comes with new life, a faith in moving forward.

The Fool stands on the edge of the cliff, readying himself to take a leap of faith, with pure intent symbolized by the white rose he holds, and supported by the highest form of spirituality, the Universal Energy, represented by the white sun in the sky. Following his heart's desire, he trusts the outcome to be in his favor.

When The Fool shows up in a reading, the inquirer is guided to have complete faith and trust that what is coming up next is the right thing to do and that he is where he's supposed to be. It could also indicate that the person is anxious to start something new or is about to begin a new cycle. These desires are being given to the person by divine will (God). Because it is karmic in nature, it will have great meaning for the person. This card encourages the person to be self-motivated and take a leap of faith. Don't wait to be pushed or forced into it.

This card represents innocence, optimism, courage, new potential, a chance to live a different way of life, and opening to the possibility of a lifetime. On the negative side, it could indicate confusion or things happening very quickly without warning, creating a situation of inadequate mental or material preparation. It may also indicate wavering, hesitation, or indiscretion.

I – The Magician

Key Words: Transformation, Power, Manifestation

The magician stands at his altar, the magical tools of his craft before him. Red and white flowers bloom around him and a lemniscate floats above his head. The lemniscate is the symbol for infinity and represents the balance of forces. The red flowers symbolize passion and the white represent purity. The tools are symbols of the elements of earth (pentacle), air (sword), fire (wand), and water (cup).

When The Magician is drawn, it is a call for the inquirer to bring in all scattered energies and focus their efforts in a directed way. This is a card of manifestation through the application of human will, intelligence, and communication. The Magician exemplifies empowerment and motivation, which are the keys to major life changes. We can create our own future. It also represents skill and the ability to demonstrate one's power.

Reversed, it indicates trickery and deception. It may also be that the inquirer does not possess the tools to accomplish the goal. The person is blocking himself from moving forward at this time.

Meditate on The Magician to cultivate motivation and internal power.

II – The High Priestess

Key Words: Intuition, Receptivity, Feminine Energies, Secret Knowledge

The High Priestess sits on a throne wearing the headdress of the Moon (Isis) and her foot rests upon a crescent moon. The association with the moon demonstrates strong intuitive and psychic abilities, receptivity, feminine energies, and change.

Pillars border her on both sides balancing light and dark, one black pillar positioned in the north with the letter B (Boaz = meaning 'in him is strength') and one white pillar positioned in the south with the letter J (Jachin = 'he establishes'). These are representative of the pillars in front of Solomon's Temple, thought to be symbolic of God's presence within the temple. Seven pomegranates decorate the wall behind her, as they decorated the pillars at Solomon's temple, representing the esoteric power of the number 7 in the study of magic, mystery, and the activation of imagination in the context of the symbolism of the pomegranate, which represents abundance, passion, happiness, potential fruitfulness, and fertility.

She holds a copy of the *Tora*, which could be the Jewish *Torah* or an anagram of Tarot; in either case, the last letter is hidden. She wears an equal-armed cross on her chest—the cross of complete truth, representing perfect balance between the masculine and feminine energies. Her robes of blue and white once again portray the ties to the moon and intuitive communication.

The card of psychic awareness and subtle energies, the High Priestess holds esoteric and secret knowledge that she may or may not reveal to those who seek her advice. It is also a card of intuitive knowing from within the self and calls the inquirer to seek understanding from within. The need for creative visualization is implied, and in order to manifest your desires, it is important to first clearly see them in your mind's eye. It could also indicate that the inquirer herself has some intuitive ability of her own or that the study of the esoteric or mysterious is in her life or should be.

III – The Empress

Key Words: Fertility, Fruitful Labor, Abundance

The Empress is a fertility card, its meaning potent in the physical, mental, emotional, and spiritual realms. She could indicate a pregnancy, fruitful labor, the coming to fruition of an idea, or the spiritual abundance that comes from opening to the divine. When The Empress shows up, things will work out in a good way. It could also warn of an unwanted pregnancy, so use caution and safe sex methods to avoid this.

Use your creative imagination to bring desires from the spiritual into the physical. Apply your passion and emotional commitment to the desire and envision yourself doing it and people congratulating you for it.

With the symbol of Venus prominently displayed in a heart next to her chair, this is a card of love, joy, and beauty. It comes to those ready to carry out their plans and use their talents. Her crown of twelve 6-pointed stars shows her mastery over the world and is symbolic of the twelve signs of the zodiac.

On the negative side, The Empress could indicate idleness, blatant sexuality, or someone who tends to get by on charm and good luck.

Use the energies of The Empress to bring your desires to fruition.

IV – The Emperor

Key Words: Control, Reason

The Emperor sits majestic on his throne decorated with ram heads, wearing a gold crown, red robes, and holding a staff that is in the shape of an ankh, the symbol of eternal life. Mountains stand behind the throne.

The rams symbolize the astrological sign of Aries, the gold crown represents reason, and the color red is for passion. The Emperor, using reason, is the bridge between the spiritual plane and the human or physical plane. This card reflects the mind's eye that is used to see internal images that are then brought into the external world. The external world is the illusion. Reason is called upon when there is a decision to change or to get a new result. Something new can be constructed when what has happened in the past is remembered.

In a reading, The Emperor is a card of control; of the need or ability to be in control of oneself and of people and situations. It also indicates the ability to make a decision and carry out the plan. There is a need to think things through and use your own power.

On the positive side, this card indicates someone who is goal-oriented, ambitious, overly confident, a workaholic, or eagle-eyed. On the negative side, it portrays someone who is ill tempered, rash, masochistic, hung up on trivial things, hard headed, or someone who needs a reality check.

V – The Hierophant

Key Words: Spirit working through the physical, Intuition

The central image on The Hierophant is a powerful religious leader seated on a throne-type chair positioned between two pillars, holding up his forefinger and middle finger on his right hand, and a gold staff in his left. He wears a crown of gold and a red robe. Two monks kneel before him, a set of crossed keys between them.

This card represents a leader dealing with earthly problems and interjecting the spiritual into the physical plane. His advice is designed to bring peace and harmony to the situation. The Divine speaks through him in a very practical way, making the holy word accessible to all.

This is a card of listening to your inner or higher self; it is speaking to you. Allow the intuitive self to come through; go with your gut on important matters. It implies a person deprived of willfulness and selfishness. The ego is released, going at the point of full connection with the Universal Energy. The ego can prompt self-destructive behavior, dragging down the vibrational level. The lower the vibrational level, the higher position the ego takes, drowning out the inner voice. Decide whether you will listen to your ego or your intuition.

It may be that the person is experiencing an inner confrontation, listening more to others than to himself. The guidance system is outside of the self. The person may be keeping too much inside and needs to let it out. Once conflict is released, it is possible to open to inspiration.

On the positive side, The Hierophant denotes a person who is solid, dependable, punctual, conventional, and traditional—not wild and crazy; could be a church-going person, or very spiritual.

On the negative side, it implies an individual who is overly scholarly or preachy, part of the moral majority, stubborn, or abusive to the personal freedom of others.

This card represents the occupations of most traditional religious vocations (priest, nun, rabbi, minister); also guru, psychotherapist, counselor, social worker, teacher, CEO and the sign of Taurus.

VI – The Lovers

Key Words: Relationship, Temptation, Body-Mind-Spirit

Archangel Raphael hovers behind a male and a female, Adam and Eve. Eve looks to the angel (super conscious), while Adam (self-conscious) looks upon Eve (subconscious). The self-conscious cannot do anything without the subconscious, because everything is made of the subconscious. The subconscious is ruled by the super conscious. The male represents self-consciousness and the female the subconscious mind, both needing to be intimately entwined in order to work together. The Tree of Knowledge behind Eve bears five fruits which represent the five senses. The tree of human life is behind Adam, its fruit representing forms of life expression and personality.

In a reading, it may be reflective of an actual relationship that has a lot going for it and speaks to the need to appreciate the differences between the two people involved in that relationship.

On an energetic level, The Lovers implies a rebirth, being born again to pure energy. There is a physical transformation to accommodate this energy and the person to whom it pertains will be able to perform miracles.

This card also represents temptation and correct decision making. It warns not to take problems personally. Look at the situation and see what you can do; don't worry about what you cannot do. Ask yourself about the rules of the game you are playing. Be open and vulnerable to what other people are about.

In a positive sense, The Lovers represents advancement over personal inertia, choices offered, decisions needed, friendship, alliance, adaptability, the need to make everything work (marriage, job), or a family meeting.

On the negative side, it could indicate the failure to meet the responsibilities toward a mate or a lack of ability to connect with the subconscious and super conscious. This could be in the present lifetime or a past life. It may point to someone who abandoned a relationship because they could not handle the responsibilities. This may reflect someone who has trouble finding a mate or who has trouble creating relationships. In this case, The Lovers calls you to adjust to the situation until you can meet it with patience and responsibility.

VII – The Chariot

Key Words: Control, Unite Opposites

The Chariot is a card of control. The horses (or sphinx in this case) are not harnessed, indicating that the charioteer is controlling them with his mind. The positive and negative energies are symbolized by the white and black sphinx respectively.

This card calls you to say aloud what you desire. Make all opposites unite. It may indicate being stuck and locked in cement, unable to move. See what is not being noticed or attended to that is keeping the person in the same place. As victory is perceived, you will be freed from the block of materiality.

This card could indicate something having to do with a vehicle or the ability to take control over a situation.

VIII – Strength

Key Words: Strength, Self-confidence

Strength indicates that true strength comes with the ability to control the subconscious mind. Suggest what you want to the subconscious and allow that which you desire to manifest as a function of investing in it emotionally, mentally, and through visualization. Be careful what you say to yourself. Don't doubt yourself; avoid using words like "but."

In a reading, Strength can signal a recovery after difficulties. It also advises not to fear facing ordeals; learn to cope with situations. If you find yourself in a place you don't want to be, reconsider your goals and answers. You may be applying your energy to the wrong aspect of the situation.

Strength calls for introspection and the promotion of self honesty to avoid misusing your natural gifts and talents. Through self-awareness, it is possible to be confident, self-assured, adaptable, and to reject temptation. This will allow you to think big rather than limiting yourself. Success demands organization. It also implies the need for self control in relationships with others. It is best to approach others with a sense of kindness and a nurturing quality in order to overcome rough times in a relationship.

On the negative side, Strength represents confusion, weakness, and not seeing the whole picture.

Use your inner and outer strength wisely.

IX – The Hermit

Key Words: Wisdom, Withdrawal, Solitude

The Hermit stands alone atop a mountain, lighting the way for those who seek wisdom and for all those who come after him. The light represents the light of the Universal Energy that brightens the heart and spirit in the darkest times. The light also symbolizes inner wisdom and knowledge. In this state, ego is no longer needed.

When The Hermit is drawn, it may be a call for you to withdraw from the situation to ponder your options. Wisdom is gained in solitude. It also may be that you are attempting to communicate an original idea and need to help others understand its implications. In this way, you light the path for others. Positive implications are associated with inner guidance; wisely and confidently executing your own decisions and having the courage of your convictions.

Reversed, it indicates misunderstanding and lack of insight. It may also point to a person who knit picks or who has poor social skills.

Meditate on The Hermit to open to messages from your higher self.

X – The Wheel of Fortune

Key Words: Wealth, Destiny, Expansion

The Wheel of Fortune hangs suspended in midair, supported by a jackal-headed human, bordered by a snake, and a creature with the head of a pharaoh on the body of a lion holding a sword perched at the top. Each corner is occupied by one of four creatures: an angel, a bull, a lion, and an eagle. Each has an astrological correspondence: the angel to Aquarius (Air), the bull to Taurus (Earth), the lion to Leo (Fire), and the eagle to Scorpio (Water). The clouds in the background, along with the blue sky and summarily all of the creatures are symbolic of the planet Jupiter. The wheel itself contains Hebrew letters, the Latin word R.O.T.A. (meaning wheel), and four alchemical symbols implying the four elements.

Because the images all support the assignment of Jupiter as this card's associated planetary influence, it represents expansive energy. In general, the Wheel of Fortune implies something good is coming, but you cannot simply wait for it. Rather, there is a need to be actively involved in the situation. Nothing will happen if you just stand there and hold out your hand.

This card also indicates someone who wants to have it all; someone who goes for the gusto in life. They live life in the fast lane and take advantage of what is offered. It may also represent someone to whom playing the game is more important than winning or losing.

As with all tarot cards, there is a duality inherent in the meaning; while the Wheel of Fortune could indicate wealth, its reverse could mean poverty or a greedy, over-materialistic person.

XI – Justice

Key Words: Truth, Justice, Karmic Balance

Justice refers to that which is fair and true, karmic justice administering consequences and rewards for the actions we take. Karma seeks to balance the scales of justice. The sword represents the power of discernment and discrimination, enabling appropriate action. The sword eliminates extraneous matter from the situation and boils circumstances down to the most basic aspects.

Justice also stands for activities within the law itself. It may represent an attorney, any type of legal action including contracts or divorce, or a court case. It could also indicate government regulation or influence. With The Devil, it may indicate incarceration.

It is a card of balance, equilibrium, the astrology sign Libra, and represents the importance of taking action toward resolution. What is coming is what will balance what came before. You are balancing your karma through choices.

XII – The Hanged Man

Key Words: Release, Connection, Relaxation

The Hanged Man is one of the top four highly misunderstood cards in the major arcana (the others being Death, The Tower, and The Devil) thanks to its portrayal in Hollywood movies and fear left over from times when hanging was the prevalent form of execution. The man in the image is not hanging from his neck, but rather from one foot with his hands resting behind his back.

This is a posture of relaxation that can be used in a prostrate position when you want to release tension. A light glows around his head indicating the divine presence. He is in a complete state of meditation; personal consciousness is suspended, and he has entered into communication with the Universal Energy.

In a reading, it implies a person who ties himself up with internal pressures, yet has the power to release himself from stress and tension through exercises such as deep breathing and yoga, as well as a change of perspective. The conflict is coming from within the self; it is advisable to surrender the perceived problems to the Universal Energy and allow guidance to come through peaceful clearing and open acceptance.

XIII – Death

Key Words: Ending, Transition, Rebirth

Probably one of the most misunderstood cards in the tarot, Death features a skeletal figure in a suit of armor on horseback, carrying a flag and, in some cases, a scythe. The white horse treads over a field of dead people, while others stand by, paying respect to those who have passed on. In the background, the sun peeks over the horizon between the familiar towers from The Moon cautioning not to separate yourself from all of the various aspects you hold within.

Death itself is a transition from one state to another. This card may denote the death of a state of being, a belief, or a situation. It could portend the ending of a relationship. The type of ending can be interpreted in the context of the cards around it. Death suggests the end of a cycle and the beginning of a new one. An ending can be positive in the light of a fresh start. To bring in new energy, a void must be created.

Remember that an ending is not necessarily a bad thing; it may be timely to your growth process. Detach from the emotionality of the situation. Be aware of the implications of what is ending and consider how the death of a particular situation, relationship, or part of yourself is necessary for you to move forward.

XIV – Temperance

Key Words: Alignment, Attainment, Harmony

An archangel stands with one foot on dry land and the other in the water, pouring liquid between two chalices. The pouring cup is higher, implying that the higher self or divine wisdom is feeding the lower cup or base nature (consciousness) of the individual. The liquid between the cups is in the form of wavy lines, representing consciousness being modified as the water is being poured from one cup to another. A yellow brick road leads to a glowing crown in the sky over the mountains in the distance, mirroring the glow around the archangel's head. A round disk appears on the forehead, symbolizing activation of the Third Eye.

One foot in each realm indicates having control of both earthly considerations and the subconscious. The radiating glow around the head and the presence of the Third Eye exemplifies that when the chakras are aligned, the Kundalini energy can move freely, energizing your entire auric field (energy body). The glowing crown in the distance symbolizing Man is crowned God—able to directly connect with the divine energy. The yellow brick road represents attainment of all earthly aspirations.

In a reading, on the positive side, this shows a person who has their life together with harmony, wholeness, calmness, and good partnerships. If they are separated from a loved one, this card indicates reconciliation; if ill, regeneration.

On the negative side, Temperance represents someone who is compartmentalized and lacks self-control. They may behave on the wild side and go to extremes. This card calls for them to be moderate and take things in stride.

XV – The Devil

Key Words: Restriction, Limitation, Materiality

The Devil is one of the top four highly misunderstood cards in the major arcana (the others being Death, The Tower, and The Hanged Man) thanks to its portrayal in Hollywood movies and fear connected with being influenced by evil forces. In reality, this card denotes the limitation and restriction that results when we lose focus of the divine energy that works through our subconscious and rather looking at the ego or self-conscious for guidance.

The Devil represents the material aspects of life that, without the balance of the Universal Energy, bind and limits us rather than opening us to leading a life of fulfillment.

In a reading, the idea of bondage through materiality speaks volumes and offers a caution to modify the way an individual views what is important in life. It may also indicate someone who is, has been, or will be incarcerated. The Devil also represents substance abuse and/or sexual activity, possibly kinky sex that includes restraints. This is the sex, drugs, and rock 'n roll card, implying a lifestyle immersed in material gain and physical pleasure.

XVI – The Tower

Key Words: Disruption, Warning, Karmic Lessons

The Tower is one of the top four highly misunderstood cards in the major arcana (the others being Death, The Devil, and The Hanged Man), thanks to its portrayal in Hollywood movies and fear connected with disruption of the status quo. This card carries the vibrations of disruption, destruction, collapse, and chaos; these serving to put an end to stagnation and to allow new energy to come in. A void must be created in order for the next phase of development to occur.

In a reading, the disruption can pertain to financial loss, job layoff, loss of residence, or any situation that is radically changed through forces beyond your control. Ultimately, the situation bears close scrutiny, as it has been put into place in order for personal growth to occur through the learning of karmic lessons; the more severe the disruption, the more critical the lesson. It may be that the Universe has been trying to send the message in more subtle ways, yet the individual chose to ignore it rather than heed the warnings that would have allowed for a more gradual transition.

The Tower is also a card of warning to be careful and vigilant in order to avoid accidents and injury.

XVII – The Star

Key Words: Hope, Accomplishment, Potential

The Star offers several messages bound in its occult symbolism. The large yellow star in the center has eight points, representing regeneration, perfection, divine nature, and the infinite. Through these vibrations, we work to align earthly and spiritual goals in order to reach our potential. The limitless nature of our potential is inherent in this card, the promise of new life or new endeavor if we open to the possibilities.

Power is derived from our mental reality, hence the yellow color of the star, symbolizing the element of Air and mental capacity and clarity. We create mental images to represent that which begins in the spiritual in order to bring it to manifestation in the physical. We are responsible for shaping our own world through our work.

The water in the image represents intuitive communication, that is, the flow of energy from the divine, to our higher self, and into the physical. With one knee on the ground and one foot on the water, the woman in the image bridges the gap between the subconscious and the conscious mind. By opening our intuition, we allow the Universe to communicate messages, which we then manifest.

In a reading, this card puts forth the vibration of hope, accomplishment, or pending achievement. This indicates the potential of what is possible, and it is important to include the need to take responsibility for what is available to us in order to reap the benefits. Additionally, this card may indicate someone who is draining their energy by ignoring divine guidance and wasting their efforts.

XVIII – The Moon

Key Words: Intuition, Cycles, Receptivity

The Moon is card XVIII in the major arcana. In a standard tarot deck, this card features a dog and a wolf baying at the moon, while a lobster or crab joins them from the water nearby. This shows the evolution from a wild wolf to a domesticated dog; and the evolution of man from the sea. There are two towers in the distance framing the scene, cautioning not to separate yourself from all of the various aspects you hold within. A combination moon/sun watches over the activity below.

The moon represents the spiritual, feminine aspect. It holds receptive energy and symbolizes intuition and psychic awareness. The combination of the sun and the moon together indicates the need to align your chakras. The moon also suggests that everything goes in cycles. The key words for The Moon are change and intuition.

In a reading, The Moon signals that you're mentally feeling like you are moving on to the next step. Things are bound to change. Utilize what you know of the situation. You cannot see it as a whole, so look at what is available to you and move on from that point. The Moon comes up when you have been in one place too long or struggling with a karmic problem. Keep treading water for a little while longer. Step back from the situation or person that you are involved with. If you are coming out of a really bad cycle, don't worry, there is something better out there. This card may also point to emotional problems, such as depression. It points to someone who is highly intuitive and to the cycles that people and situations go through.

XIX – The Sun

Key Words: Energy, Happiness, Motivation

This is a card of high energy and happiness. The white horse represents purity and the nude child atop the horse symbolizes the innocence of childhood where anything is possible. The light and heat from the sun feed our bodies and our spirits. It represents the masculine projective energy that makes us strong and propels us forward.

In a reading, The Sun represents renewed energy and motivation toward goals. It symbolizes the bright prospects that are before the inquirer or a fresh start, especially after a time of difficulty. This high energy allows for mental clarity; it is the energy that results from the alignment of the chakras.

In some readings, The Sun may denote a vacation to a warm climate, or if a move is indicated, relocation to a warm climate.

XX – Judgement

Key Words: Final Result, Completion, Decision

Judgement shows an image in which Archangel Gabriel sounds the trumpet that creates the vibration of listening to your inner voice in projecting what you want. Through recognizing inner guidance, the individual is empowered to transform into the true self. This is also a karmic card, indicating that the person has mastered their previous incarnations and is now in their final lifetime on the physical plane.

The equal armed cross on the flag, which predates the Christian cross, symbolizes the balance of elemental energies (earth, air, fire, and water), that of the natural union of male and female, and of the four seasons. It is the cross of truth in that all suffering is a result of human action, and final judgment will be at the hand of Karma, which balances and levels the action with appropriate rewards or consequences.

In a reading, Judgement is a card of completion and of attainment, signifying a cycle coming to an end. Whatever is in the person's life was chosen by no one but himself, and now he must take command of the situation through choosing right action and ultimately learning through experience, and from the interactions with those around him. It may also imply someone who is judgmental toward others and who needs to pay more attention to how he himself impacts others, as well as what can be learned from them.

XXI – The World

Key Words: Growth, Direct Energy, Success

The World signifies gaining control over the self and the environment. The wreath indicates the growth that has been achieved in the external realm, while the blue sash symbolizes understanding gained through intuition. The wands she holds indicate her ability to direct the energy available to her toward whatever she chooses.

As with The Wheel of Fortune, once again each corner is occupied by one of four creatures: an angel/man, a bull, a lion, and an eagle. Each of them has an astrological correspondence: the angel to Aquarius (Air), the bull to Taurus (Earth), the lion to Leo (Fire), and the eagle to Scorpio (Water).

In a reading, The World indicates that the person has come fully into herself and recognizes the value she brings to the world. It is a card of success and of changes made as a result of taking all the knowledge gained over a lifetime and channeling it for the greater good as well as for the highest good of the self.

7   The Minor Arcana

Aces

Ace of Cups

Key Words: Emotional fulfillment, one year

The Ace of Cups is the emotional fulfillment card. When it shows up in a reading, expect wonderful things to happen that will promote contentment and abundance. "Your cup runneth over" is a good phrase to attach to this card.

The white dove represents spirit and the water lilies symbolize thoughts, yet have grounding in the material world. With spirit working through the mind and fueled by emotion, good things will come to you. Be open and accepting of what is coming.

The Ace of Cups may also indicate leaks in the house or something overflowing. It also denotes that whatever is coming will be here within one week, one month, or one year.

Ace of Pentacles

Key Words: Money, Values, One Year

The Ace of Pentacles denotes money or values. The pentagram in the upright position appears as a man's head, two arms, and two legs. Upright, it symbolizes spirit over the material, while the inverted represents the material controlling or taking precedent over spirit; hence its association with the devil with two horns, ears, and chin. This could imply that the person's desire is being forced from the spiritual to the material.

The path on the card is the yellow brick road, which stands for insight, but the kind of insight that you have worked out over a period of time. The path will lead to spiritual and material aspirations. A lot of thought and planning is involved. This card can signal the beginning of self-expression.

The Ace of Pentacles could also mean something new, like a new job, a wedding or engagement ring, or a move. This could be a move of residence or a moving of the work location.

Ace of Swords

Key Words: Decision, Separation, One Year

The image shows a crown floating in the air, denoting man and his ability to think. It also means going to the highest spiritual plane. The laurel on the left and palm on the right represents the feminine-masculine/passive-active energies respectively. The sword in the air indicates mentality."

The Ace of Swords is a card of major decisions. As with all aces, it denotes a period of one year. When drawing this card, it may be that you will be making an important decision within the next 12 months.

Another interpretation of the Ace of Swords is a person having a brilliant thought; that sense of expanded awareness that brings forth an "aha" moment after puzzling over a problem and getting an answer.

It could also be some kind of split-up. What used to be together has been separated and you must use your power to bring it back together. Swords represent conflict or sickness, so the Ace of Swords may point to the initial part of a cure or finding a doctor. It could also warn of something sharp.

Ace of Wands

Key Words: Career, Goals, One Year

The Ace of Wands is the best career card in the deck. The inquirer will be using his or her skills and abilities to accomplish much in the next 12 months. This card also denotes the initiation or beginning of something. There could be growth in skills or talents.

It could also mean creating something out of nothing. The Ace of Wands represents what the inquirer will ultimately do. With the hand emerging from the cloud, it means creating something out of nothing or out of the blue. The person could also be making or doing something to further his or her career or to work toward a goal.

Two (II)

II of Cups

Key Words: Relationships, Respect, Partnership

The Two of Cups is the best relationship card in the deck. It denotes a mutual giving and receiving and respect for one another. This can apply to friendships, romantic relationships, or other types of partnerships. The winged lion denotes spirituality and the entwined snakes represent attraction.

There is dignity in this relationship; an even exchange. This affords transformational energy and healing actions. It could be that the person is coming into a new relationship with whom he has a lot in common.

When the Two of Cups comes up, be confident that it indicates a stable relationship that will work if you give the best of yourself to the other person. This union will create a balanced energy between two people (or entities/businesses).

II of Pentacles

Key Words: Stagnation, Indecision, Delay

The traditional image of the Two of Pentacles depicts a young male seemingly juggling two pentacles encased in an elongated lemniscate, the symbol for infinity. Each hand holds one of the pentacles. In the background, the sky is pale blue and calm, and the sea is rough; two ships navigating the huge waves of the ocean.

Because the water is turbulent and the hands are juggling, it implies that there is desire, but it is not channeled in the right place. The person is trying to make a decision and everything turns chaotic. It portrays a sense of making a mess of the situation. The person is under a strain because of a decision. It could be financial juggling.

The person is thinking in terms of either/or rather than a potential solution of a combination of two possibilities. Or they may be faced with two options that are equally good, and they may have to pursue both things.

It may indicate that the person is working two jobs and is stressed out because of it. They may be making a major life decision or change. The stress is a result of the person's action or inaction; he is creating the stress himself. Or he could be a victim of a situation.

The person is trying to move toward a goal or rectify a situation, but is not making any progress. Sometimes a delay proves beneficial, and so the stagnation is not necessarily the cause for worry in this case. There will be growth from the waiting due to the realization that they must make a decision in order to effectuate change.

From a health perspective, this could indicate strain in the neck and shoulder area. It could also mean the person is so tense that they may not even realize it. It could also mean a gift of jewelry, especially a bracelet.

The Two of Pentacles counsels not to get caught up in the action. Step back and look at what's happening; look at your values. Ask yourself which way you really want to go.

II of Swords

Key Words: Mild Anxiety, Inner Conflict

The Two of Swords depicts a blindfolded woman sitting on a bench near the sea, her arms crossed over her heart chakra, holding a sword in each hand. This denotes that she is defending herself against her imagination. The moon has risen behind her. The cube upon which she sits denotes materiality or the real world. The points of the swords are outside of the picture, indicating that the problem is all in her head.

This card comes up when the inquirer is experiencing some anxiety about a situation. They are emotionally uncomfortable and may also be having physical symptoms such as headaches as a result of the anxiety. The Two of Swords indicates real discomfort, unhappiness, a tendency to guard oneself, and that the person may be completely blind to what's going on.

They spend too much time worrying and making the problem bigger. The problem that is worrying this person is not real; all she has to do is put down the swords and remove the blindfold.

The Two of Swords can also indicate a relationship in a state of conflict. It may be that the person is seeing two people and feeling guilty about it, or can't make up their mind about which one to be with. It could also be the inquirer's relationship with herself, feeling hurt, being in the process of making a decision, being defensive, or feeling a sense of guilt. It could be anything that is going on inside the person's head. The person may be thinking about starting an argument with someone.

The inquirer may be over-prepared, defensive, and vulnerable. This person has a choice to make: put down the swords or continue to be unhappy. What is going on in her head will materialize in the real world if she keeps on the same track.

This person is also closing themselves off from others. The Two of Swords is calling the inquirer to be more open and share what is going on inside of them with other people. The person thinks everyone is a mind reader and should know what is happening with her without her saying anything.

II of Wands

Key Words: Crossroads, Uncertainty, Desire

The Two of Wands shows a man looking out into the world, wondering what to do next. He wears the red cap of desire. He's looking to conquer the world, but there is more to do. The staffs in the picture are stationary, meaning no growth. He may be getting advice from many people on the one hand, and, on the other, has ideas of his own. The Two of Wands indicates the need to get clear on taking the next step because you want to, not because someone else says you should.

There is an uncertainty about movement associated with this card. The person is at a crossroads. There is a sense of knowing that there is something better out there, but no steps have been taken to get it; desire without action. It's important to use your skills and talents to figure out what to do next.

This period of non-growth is only temporary. This period leads to growth and productivity in the future. There is desire and spirituality. Now is the time to plant the seeds and get the necessary development, but no decision has been made yet. Ask if you just want to settle for what is currently in your life or if you want something beyond that. Then take the necessary steps to get it.

Three (III)

III of Cups

Key Words: Celebration, Wedding, Happiness

Three women hold up goblets in a toast as they dance in a circle, the fruits of harvest on the ground around them and a sprig of grapes held by one of the women, symbolizing abundance. The garment colors signify purity (white), energy (orange), and mental clarity or intelligence (yellow).

This is a card of celebration. It could portend a wedding, engagement, or some other major reason to have a party. The III of Cups promotes positive feelings of self-worth or self-value. It calls for you to be nicer to yourself.

The III of Cups also indicates getting the fruits of your labor. Expect a happy occasion when this card shows up.

III of Pentacles

Key Words: Group, Construction, Support

The Three of Pentacles is the card of people working together. It may be a cohesive group or people coming together from several different places. It can denote things of a vocational nature such as unions, labor relations, someone who is a builder or architect, or in the construction arts; anyone who works in any of the trades.

It can also indicate someone who has a plan that he will have support for or need help executing.

III of Swords

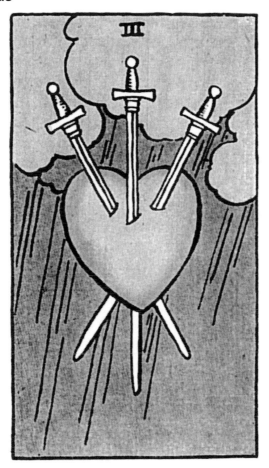

Key words: Heartbreak, Grudge, Emotional Pain

The Three of Swords comes up when there has been or will be heartbreak. It could pertain to a relationship or a situation. If the emotional pain has occurred in the past, it is important to take a look at what caused it to avoid it happening the same way in the future.

Now that the swords have plunged through the heart, the tips of the blades are no longer as sharp as they were at first. This is an indication that things will improve from this point forward. The worst is over.

This card can also mean that the person has gone through some really rough relationships or has a history of bad relationships. It could indicate a person who is inadequate at solving his own problems or someone who is easily overwhelmed. It's best to move slowly and cautiously in making decisions.

This may also represent a person who holds a grudge or who is nasty or says nasty things. This bad attitude and behavior require a change to avoid getting into trouble. They create their own problems. The problems can be solved, but they must take responsibility for the situation.

III of Wands

Key Words: Readiness, Growth, Movement

A man stands on a cliff overlooking a calm sea. Only his back can be seen. Boats float gently on the water below. He holds a staff in one hand and is bordered by two others stuck firmly in the ground, all with leaves growing from them.

This image shows that the seeds (rods, staffs, wands) have been planted and they are growing. The wands could represent skills, ideas, or goals that are growing and coming to fruition. He is ready to move forward toward achievement and accomplishment of his desired task.

The III of Wands could denote someone whose ship is coming in, but once the ship leaves the dock, he is no longer in control. It is important to get new activities going while putting the things you have control over out of your mind.

This is also a person who wants to find out what else there is in life and is ready to move beyond where he has been.

The III of Wands could also mean that there are three people in a situation. The person is leaning more towards one than the other two. It represents someone who may be detached from their surroundings or relationships. This could be someone who may be getting a position as a leader or is a supervisor of other people.

Another interpretation could be that the person is suffering from "empty nest syndrome" or his or her kids are in their first year of school and they are alone.

This card also indicates that the person is holding onto one skill and should expand their skills and find new things to do. They may be at a dead end and should look to something new. They need some excitement in their life. There is a lot of desire and creativity surrounding the situation or person—it is coming from the spiritual into the material. Something has to be brought to their attention. Turn around and look at things from a different perspective.

IV of Cups

Key Words: Choices, Decision, Ideas

The IV of Cups is a decision-making card. The image portrays a man sitting before three cups on the ground with one coming out of thin air. The cups represent his choices or what he perceives as his alternatives. He has only considered the mundane or earthly options at this point, since Spirit is offering another choice. It is important that this alternative be taken seriously and not pushed aside as impossible. There are several options before him, and he needs to pick one. If it doesn't work, then he can choose another one.

The cup coming out of the cloud may also indicate that something new is entering the picture, like a person or a situation that changes the landscape of what is being considered.

With arms folded, the man is closed to the potential of the new idea, person, or situation, and must open in order to make the best decision. He needs to see that there is another way to look at or solve the problem. This card will come up for a person who has tunnel vision; who doesn't want to make a decision; who has trouble making a decision; or who is afraid to make a decision. This stance puts him in limbo about making a choice. It may also be that the person thinks he has all his bases covered but doesn't and needs to reevaluate the situation to confirm what he should do.

Rather than refusing to take action or make a choice, it is better to make a choice, follow that road, and see where it leads. If the person is afraid to move forward, whatever happens as a result of the choice probably will not be half as bad as he thinks. It's good to have many alternatives rather than limited options.

In a relationship reading, it could be that one of the parties involved is unable or unwilling to make a commitment or afraid of making a commitment. If a decision is not made soon, s/he could lose the other person.

IV of Pentacles

Key Words: Control, Details, Limitation

The IV of Pentacles denotes a person who stays on top of the details or many tasks simultaneously, not letting anything fall through the cracks. It could also indicate a person who is controlling in situations or who is stingy with their money. It may be the case that the person only has enough money to pay their bills and nothing extra.

The person is weighed down by trying to keep too many tasks or issues under his control. It's time to put down the pentacles and take a look at the situation without these limitations. By trying to control everything, and by intellectualizing and categorizing tasks, responsibilities, and issues, he is limiting himself from seeing past what is right under his nose. Encourage the person to branch out in new directions—whether it's materially, mentally, spiritually, or emotionally—to break the pattern of limitation.

IV of Swords

Key Words: Insomnia, Rest

The IV of Swords is a card of sleep problems: insomnia, waking up in the middle of the night. The image of a man laying on a platform surrounded by swords may also indicate a person resting from having to make a decision. The swords represent conflicts within the person; it's in his head and causing problems on the material plane.

This could also indicate someone who negatively imagines things, so negatively creates his or her reality.

Suggest quiet contemplation to allow the person to visualize fresh beginnings. There is a solution, and the person needs to open to the answers available to him.

IV of Wands

Key Words: Faith, Self-reliance

Four rods stand in the ground, standing two together and draped with a garland of flowers. Revelers wave bunches of flowers above their heads in celebration before a large white castle. The yellow background represents the element of Air and mental ability.

This is a card of faith; have faith in yourself and in the idea that things will work out for the best. Rely on your own skills and positive attitude. Don't be afraid to trust yourself. Be open and trusting about the situation and about your power in the situation. You are strong enough to handle whatever is in your life right now; you don't need protection.

This card may come up when a person feels vulnerable or is in a vulnerable situation. Don't fear the worst.

V of Cups

Key Words: Despair, Grief, Loss

The Five of Cups is a card of despair, yet it does not have to be. This is the "don't cry over spilled milk" card. The image shows a man in a black cape focusing on the three spilled cups and ignoring the two full cups standing just behind him. He is choosing to take the negative mindset and wraps himself in a shroud of black to demonstrate his dark mood.

Other interpretations of this card include the indication of grief or depression. The person has lost something emotionally. The loss may not be in reality, but rather in the mind. It could be that the person is living in the past or concentrating too much on one thing or one direction.

A change of perspective is what is needed here. There are alternatives waiting to be discovered as symbolized by the two upright cups. Additionally, there is a river just feet away to refill the spilled cups. Focus on the positive aspects of the situation and take off the cape of darkness to lighten up.

When the Five of Cups comes up, take heart; there is a way out of the problem or situation. Whatever is happening, it is only temporary or indicates a short-term loss. The house in the background indicates that the solution to the problem may be found in the person's environment, where he lives, works, or plays. The key is to do something, anything, rather than give up.

Five (V)

V of Pentacles

Key Words: Depression, Self-pity, Suffering

The traditional image of the Five of Pentacles shows two people trudging through the snow. The female in the image wears a tattered shawl that she has draped over her head and clutches around her neck to fend off the cold, and a male with one bandaged foot on crutches. They are walking by a church window with the pentacles displayed in a Tree of Life formation on the stained glass.

This card indicates a person or persons with a poor self-image. They pity themselves and wallow in their self-imposed suffering. They are not looking for help and they buy in to their own delusions. This card can also indicate someone who is depressed and having trouble pulling out of the slump.

The message brought by the Five of Pentacles is to heal yourself. Do not be afraid to address your issues and to let go of your bad self-image. Use visualization, self-expression, and creativity to make a better life for yourself. If in a period of strife, it is important to clarify your objectives and determine what you value most in your situation.

V of Swords

Key Words: Gloating Winner, Battle, Compromise

A man stands holding three swords with two lying on the ground at his feet. The grin on his face indicates that he has won the battle as his adversaries walk away in defeat. This person is gloating over his victory. Did he really need to defeat his opponents summarily or could he have taken a stance of partial triumph and left them with their dignity? How many swords did he need to use to win the battle?

The battle has been won, but the war may have been lost. There is no room for compromise with those who have been devastated by these actions. One-upmanship is a self-serving strategy, chosen by those who may have been stripped of their self-worth in the past.

This card could also indicate someone who is prejudiced or a victim of prejudice. Possibly someone who was shamed as a child or who has lost an election. Something happened in public that brought shame or what the person is ashamed of.

To repair the damage, change perspective and get something new going. Use your skills to positive advantage and help others feel equal again. This could also mean that ideas that were previously accepted may now have to be rejected.

V of Wands

Key Words: Networking, Practice, Action

The Five of Wands is a card of networking. It calls you to get into the fray, into the action. Don't stand idly by and miss an opportunity. It indicates doing something that will help later on, like a skill you've been practicing.

This card is one that shows the expression of energy. You can also look for initials in this card (X, A, H). There could be a new person in town.

Another interpretation could be that you may feel outnumbered and a little on the defensive. It may be that you are in a new situation or one you don't want to be in. It may indicate people who you don't want to be with or having to go to a party with people you don't want to be around.

The situation allows you to bring new energy and to help others release energy.

VI of Cups

Key Words: Two-faced, Playfulness

The Six of Cups is an innocent looking card; yet, on closer inspection, it shows that the girl is not necessarily open to accepting what the boy is offering her. There is a chance that the person behaves toward her in a positive way in her presence and talks about her when he is away; a two-faced person. This card calls for the inquirer to determine if the person is being upfront or not.

In a relationship reading, it may be that an affair is tarnishing the relationship. It may also be that one person does everything for the other with no reciprocation, or one person may not be able to make a commitment.

On the lighter side, the Six of Cups denotes recreation, outdoor activity, and playfulness. It could also indicate someone who is or was a hippie or flower child.

VI of Pentacles

Key Words: Giving, Financial Caution

The Six of Pentacles displays a man handing money to beggars on the one hand and holding a scale in the other. His red coat is an indication of his passion and the hat designates the need to give thought to his actions.

From a monetary perspective, this card indicates that the situation may result in more money going out than coming in, but the scales show that the accounts are likely to be balanced in the end. It also indicates that there is more need than there is available funding.

Another aspect of the Six of Pentacles is that it is a card of values. If the inquirer is wondering how to divide his energy, time, or money, this card calls him to ask who can use more of what he is giving. It also cautions the inquirer to be careful of what is given out; do not give all of what you have—save some for yourself. It may be that the person is giving too much in a relationship or maybe that someone does not need what you have to give them, like advice.

This card could denote relationship or divorce problems, as the scales are symbolic of justice or the legal system. Justice does not mean equality, it means getting what is deserved. The scales may also represent karmic justice. You will get what you need if you ask for it; do not expect people to read your mind. Look at your inner requirements, not just material needs.

VI of Swords

Key Words: Temporary Conflict

The Six of Swords is the temporary conflict card. Move forward slowly, let things ride, and don't mess with the issues (swords) prematurely; otherwise, you may sink the boat. Even though there is conflict surrounding what is happening, the person is moving in the right direction and will ultimately pass through the situation.

VI of Wands

Key Words: Success, Leadership

The Six of Wands is a card of success. The person has risen above his current work status to become a supervisor, manager, or leader of some kind. He carries the wreath of victory and wears a green leaved wreath on his head, indicating status, money, and success.

For there to be a leader, there must also be followers, and so it is important that this person think positively about group dynamics and be aware of the needs of those who report to him. The message here is not to outdistance those who support you, but rather stay with the foot soldiers.

This card also indicates the need to be a spokesman for the group or possibly committee work.

VII of Cups

Key Words: Unlimited Potential, Choices

The Seven of Cups is the card of unlimited potential. The image shows a person in shadow standing before seven golden cups, each holding an object that represents a path or potentiality. The objects in the cups are as follows, along with their meanings:

- Castle or mountain – Urge or search for worldly power (business, etc.). Also denotes the Black Arts.

- Head or rainbow – Beauty

- Mask, stars, or ghostly image – Mystical or spiritual quest

- Snake or squid – In search of wisdom for their own sake. The search is valuable no matter where it leads you.

- Dragon – Power of manipulation
- Jewels – Wealth
- Laurel wreath or skull – Fame or honor. What you leave behind in the world.

Generally, the Seven of Cups means that in some way or some manner, you have reached adult status and can pick and choose your own cup or cups when you want to. There are choices having to do with self-knowledge or spiritual awakening. It may also indicate that you are ultra-material in your approach to the world. An alternate meaning is someone who is looking for what they want to do in life.

Ultimately, this card represents the ultimate potential of the person and that the world is open to them. All they need do is choose a path.

VII of Pentacles

Key Words: Contemplation, Nostalgia, The Past

A man takes a break from his work, seemingly to contemplate his life and the past. The VII of Pentacles is a minor arcane card that represents contemplation and being nostalgic. It could indicate someone who is completely immersed in memories of the past or who is living in the past rather than the present. This person must decide whether to focus on his past accomplishments or to move forward and get a new game plan going for the future.

This card could also represent someone who is thinking of a change in career. This card encourages the inquirer to look at all aspects of a situation as they ponder their next move. It could also indicate someone who loves antiques or who is thinking about past relationships or rekindling an old flame.

VII of Swords

Key Words: Betrayal, Theft, Dishonesty

The VII of Swords is the betrayal card. It denotes a thief, a dishonest person, or someone who is untrustworthy. It could also indicate someone who has trust issues.

It could also mean that if you rush through when making a plan, something may be left out or left behind. When the plan is carried out, remember discipline, command, and courage. The VII of Swords may mean the need for ambition.

Take caution when the card shows up and trust your intuition if there is worry that there may be dishonesty afoot.

VII of Wands

Key Words: Determination, Denial, Defensive

The VII of Wands is a card of physical activity. The person gripping the wand diagonally across his chest is expressing determination against all odds and has knowledge of working to succeed in the world. This card has the vibration of knowledge applied to your skills.

This card will come up for a person who asks for a reading, and then denies everything you say. The same person asks others for advice and then guards themselves against it. They defend themselves against what they perceive as criticism. Offer the suggestion that they may want to bless the intent of the message he is being given even though he does not embrace it. This person is worn out from taking a defensive position for too long.

The VII of Wands could also indicate wanting to do something useful with the odds going against him. This person has to be the best and have the shoulder of others to cry on. By doing this, he may push others away.

Another possibility is that they may be thinking about moving and may need to share their space with someone else.

VIII of Cups

Key Words: Search, Long Journey, Counseling

A person holding a walking staff walks away from eight golden cups into the wilderness, the moon shining bright above him. The person is going in search of what is missing. The cycle of searching has begun and perhaps what the person is looking for may not be found or happen right away. This means that they should take time to find out what is missing in their life and then build the foundation by doing and learning things to keep growing.

It could be that the person is abandoning his current situation as in desertion or separation, but may ultimately attempt reconciliation. If the inquirer is asking about a new partner or relationship, it will not result in a commitment or it could mean a one-sided relationship with no deep involvement. The person may not be aware of what they need. Do they need to move, change their diet, change their job, or rearrange something in their life?

This is a card of counseling and of long-term effects. One implication could be that there is a situation in need of long-term therapy (marriage, child, etc). If the VIII of Cups shows up with The Devil, it could indicate rehab for drug or alcohol abuse, or a stay at a mental hospital.

The VIII of Cups could also indicate someone who is searching for something they lost. With the II of Pentacles, they lost jewelry or money; with the IV of Pentacles, they lost car keys; Ace of Pentacles, house keys. Look to see where they'll find it (indoors, outdoors, near water, etc).

VIII of Pentacles

Key Words: Expertise, Mastery, Training

The Eight of Pentacles is a card of mastery and the development of expertise. When this card comes up, the person is studying, writing, researching, or carving themselves a place in the world, using their special gifts and talents. The person may be in a training program or an apprentice. They are studying something special. Whatever they are doing, they are working on a masterpiece.

It could also denote an artist or artisan. The person will be successful or has already experienced wonderful success with what they are doing; they are, or will be, prolific with their creations. The person is multi-talented, multi-faceted, learns quickly, and sets his own standards.

VIII of Swords

Key Words: High Anxiety, Stress, Physical Illness

The Eight of Swords is a high anxiety card. The person gets so stressed that it manifests physically as stomach aches, digestive problems, and headaches. It could also indicate medical issues such as respiratory illness, sinus problems, eye issues, lower bowel, or intestinal problems.

The person is tied up and bound, but the imprisonment may be a function of the mind or the body. It is only temporary and can be treated if physical, or changed as a result of modifying the person's mindset.

The Eight of Swords will come up for a person who is literally or figuratively paralyzed. It may indicate someone who does not want to know or see the truth; she does not want to face reality. This person's conflicts are acting out on her body (ulcers, diarrhea). She must relax lest she "kill" herself with her own worries.

Even though the person is bound up, none of the binding is tight; they could wiggle and get it off or pick up a sword and cut off the binding. This demonstrates the likelihood that the person is doing it to herself. It could be that she is having a rough time making a decision or that she has a lot of stuff going on in her head. She tends to be crushed when people are critical and takes problems personally. The solution is to make a decision or learn to shrug off issues that arise and not take everything so seriously.

VIII of Wands

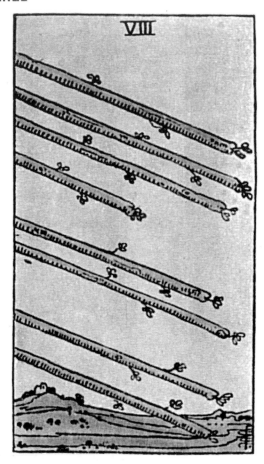

Key Words: Agitation, Messages

The Eight of Wands is a card of electricity, agitation, and "wired" energy. It could denote actual electrical issues in a house or a state of mind that is highly agitated. A state of expectation and the excitement that is felt right before something happens is a message of this card saying, "Get ready, it's coming real soon!"

It could denote news or messages in writing. Another possible indication is car problems involving pistons, spark plugs, valve taps, or something having to do with the electrical system.

Nine (IX)

IX of Cups

Key Words: Wishes Fulfilled, Manifestation

The Nine of Cups is the card of wish fulfillment; the vibration of manifesting your desires is strong at this time. While this portends good news for the attainment of your dreams, it carries with it a cautionary message to be careful what you wish for.

This card urges you to be clear about what it is you want. There are times when a delay proves more advantageous than pushing for a certain outcome. Forcing your hand in a certain direction rather than allowing divine will to determine the best course can create unforeseen effects and consequences.

IX of Pentacles

Key Words: Karma, Money, Higher Understanding

The Nine of Pentacles is a karmic card, indicating the fruition of rewards and connections as a result of actions taken in this life or in past lives. The snail leaving a trail at the bottom of the card represents the Akashic Record, the book St. Peter holds at the gate of Heaven containing a record of everything that has ever been done in the past, present, or will be done in the future. The inquirer may owe someone something in this lifetime or someone may owe the inquirer; in either case, karmic debt is at work.

The falcon means God (Spirit) helps those who help themselves; be careful stepping into someone else's path under the guise of help. The person may not want your help or you may be preventing them from learning certain lessons by intervening.

This card indicates a higher understanding of values and the person who draws this card is obliged to act accordingly. It may denote that the person sets high standards for other people and must meet those same standards in his own life.

It is also a card of money, coming as a result of a lottery win, a tax refund, or a windfall of some type.

IX of Swords

Key Words: Negative Thoughts, Difficult Cycle

The Nine of Swords is a card holding the vibrations of negative automatic thoughts, the kind that come through when you're drifting off to sleep or trying to relax. Take control of these thoughts and dispel them to regain internal peace and balance. Do not act against the thoughts, but consider what could be driving them; once understanding about the conflict is attained, the thoughts will dissipate.

This card will come up when a person is going through a cycle they desperately want to end and are taking it very hard. There is a sense of drama about the situation. This is not the time to straighten things out; the old cycle is not over yet and continues to create a sense of limbo and frustration with what is going on.

IX of Wands

Key Words: Overwhelmed, Defensive

The wands (or rods) surround a man who looks exhausted and injured, as though having been in a fight. It appears the person did not defend himself too well. The wands tower over his head, symbolizing a sense of being overwhelmed or that he has built a barricade with his skills. He has built a powerful structure that has become a defense for him.

Since the man in the image has a bandaged head and frustrated look on his face, this card implies a negative connotation. The skills he chose to defend himself with were not his strongest or best. It made him most vulnerable to attack. This card indicates that the inquirer may be feeling defensive; ask if s/he has been feeling defensive and to look at the reasons.

The person may also feel overwhelmed with too much going on around them. The person needs to work on one or two things at a time rather than try to deal with everything at once.

Ten (X)

X of Cups

Key Words: Happiness

A couple stands facing a rainbow in the sky decorated by ten golden chalices. The man has his arm around the waste of the woman, his other arm extended outward as is hers. Two children play ring-around-the-rosy nearby. The sky is clear except for the rainbow and there is a creek meandering through the meadow close by.

This is the happy, happy, happy card. All is going well and whatever is coming your way will bring joy. This card represents deep feelings, emotions, and happiness. It will sometimes come up when a person is thinking of investing in something—either an investment of energy, time, or money. It is happiness that you will be able to share with others.

X of Pentacles

Key Words: Out of Control, Philosophical Differences

The Ten of Pentacles denotes many aspects of one's life swirling about him out of his control. It also indicates a person who is vacillating about various issues he needs to contend with.

The dogs in the image symbolize fidelity and the bearded man represents Merlin the magician, a spiritual being.

Alternatively, this card can also point to those who are involved in a relationship with someone whose lifestyle, point of view, and/or philosophy of life are totally different from their own. It is important to find common goals within the relationship. Be flexible and then reconcile differences. See the other person's point of view.

This could also extend to meaning two sides of the same person.

X of Swords

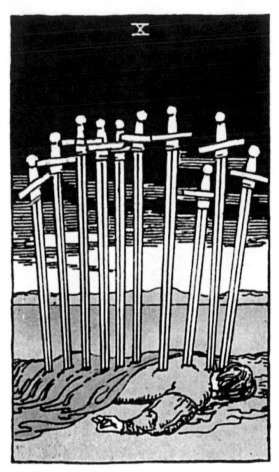

Key Words: Physical Injury, Harm

The Ten of Swords indicates either severe physical issues, such as bad back or neck pain, or a more figurative "stabbing in the back" by others. It is a cautionary card for those who are not currently experiencing any problems to be careful when lifting or to be vigilant to any activity that could create physical injury. Beware of people who may wish you harm, for their actions could cause conflicts through no fault of yours.

X of Wands

Key Words: Burden, Hard Work

The Ten of Wands is a card of burden, taking on too much and bending under the pressure. It can also indicate that the person is not using his skills to his best advantage; rethinking his approach could reduce his tension. Make new goals and plans and market your best skills

It's time to unburden yourself; pick and choose the tasks you take on rather than over-committing your life or talents. This is a person who works hard, but without proper planning, will not move him forward.

8   The Court Cards

Pages

Page of Cups

Key Words: Emotional, Drama, Artistic

The Page of Cups denotes a person who is quite emotional, a drama queen, and who may be homosexual. With the reverse, it may indicate someone who displays emotional poise. This person may also be poetic or artistic in some way. They may have some intuitive ability as indicated by the small circle on the hat, which represents the Third Eye.

Page of Pentacles

Key Words: Philosophical, Supportive

The Page of Pentacles takes a philosophical and spiritual view of life. This person tends to be idealistic and follows their dreams. Money will most likely be earned through work that incorporates counseling, inspirational, or supportive types of activities. The Page of Pentacles is a good person to consult when looking for a philosophical perspective. It may also denote a child who displays characteristics and understanding beyond their years; that of an old soul.

Page of Swords

Key Words: Desire, Vulnerability

The Page of Swords represents a person who is trying to prove him or herself, demonstrating that they are ready to be a knight. This person does not tend to use intuition or skill in the development process, but rather must learn through experience. There is great desire, but a lack of maturity, making this person vulnerable to criticism and disappointment.

Page of Wands

Key Words: Seeker, Quest

The Page of Wands represents an individual who is on a spiritual path, seeking out their particular gifts and talents in this lifetime. The person is dedicated to a task and is on a quest to discover the best ways to accomplish it.

This card denotes release of potential, so the person should be encouraged to dedicate him or herself to something, take calculated risks, and to move forward with whatever they are doing. The journey being embarked upon generally implies a long-term commitment which will require a lot of work.

Knights

Knight of Cups

Key Words: Hesitation, Lack of Commitment

The Knight of Cups represents the type of person who hesitates before taking action. He will think a decision through a little too thoroughly; causing him to procrastinate for fear that he may spill what he has already accumulated in his cup. This Knight waits for a sign, a message, or for something specific to happen before proceeding.

In a relationship reading, this is a male who has difficulty committing. He may have never been in a relationship out of fear or was in a relationship and it turned out badly; therefore, he is unwilling to commit to anyone at this time. This person may also feel unworthy of having a good relationship.

Ultimately, the individual represented by the Knight of Cups is experiencing a delay in activity and emotions and needs confidence or inspiration to be able to move forward.

Knight of Pentacles

Key Words: Loner, Temporary

The Knight of Pentacles indicates a loner, someone who comes into your life temporarily and goes back out. It could imply a quickie relationship, a one-night stand, or someone who briefly touches your life.

The Knight of Pentacles could also be a person who comes along to shed light on a situation. It may also indicate someone who is getting ready to make a contribution or to find their niche in life.

Negative attributes of this card would be a person who is on the stodgy side or a little rigid.

Knight of Swords

Key Words: Aggressive, Unfocused

The Knight of Swords is an aggressive individual, hyper, wired, and unfocused. This person takes action before thinking the decision through. He is the kind of person that makes you nervous when he comes within ten feet of you. It may also indicate a gung-ho person who is ready to take action at a moment's notice.

When this card comes up, ask the inquirer to consider grounding to get a calmer perspective or to slow down and look at the options before taking action.

Knight of Wands

Key Words: Planner, Action

The Knight of Wands represents a man who knows what he wants and has a plan to attain it. He uses his skills appropriately and will take the necessary actions to be successful. This man usually has the next opportunity lined up and does not hesitate to accomplish what he has set his mind on.

Queens

Queen of Cups

Key Words: Worrier, Anxiety, Fear

The Queen of Cups sits on a throne and holds a chalice. She represents someone who is afraid to see what is going on. She pretends it is not happening.

This card comes up when there is someone who is a worrier, always asking "What if this happens? What if that happens?" They "what if" everything and prepare for things that may never happen. Consider who in the reading, whether the inquirer or someone else pertinent to the reading, has a tendency toward anxiety as a result of worrying about the future.

This card calls for an examination of the situation and all its aspects in order to dispel fear and know what it is that needs to be dealt with.

Queen of Pentacles

Key Words: Luxury, Nurturing, Spiritual Guidance

The Queen of Pentacles can be down to earth or one who likes living a luxurious lifestyle. There is a tendency to do for others and neglects giving herself the same attention. She needs to focus on the things that are important to her as an individual, as well as providing support to others.

This card can denote a woman who has a calming influence on others or who may be taking medication to stay calm. It may be that she takes a highly spiritual approach to situations rather than approaching them from a more grounded perspective.

Queen of Swords

Key Words: Decision, Change

The Queen of Swords holds the sword of discrimination. She is able to make a decision or determination among choices by cutting away emotionality and drama and getting to the core of the matter. The opposite characteristic denoted by this card is a person having the trait of ambivalence or tunnel vision; unable to make a decision or not taking all pertinent information into consideration.

Her crown of butterflies denotes a person in the middle of a metamorphosis or in the middle of a change. This can imply an internal change as in modifying or cutting away a particular belief or deciding on new goals or it can indicate an external change such as quitting smoking or changing eating habits. Either way, there is a rebirth of some type as a result of the changes. It may feel like it is taking a long time to come to fruition, but it will be worth it in the end.

This card can also stand for a woman who is having trouble conceiving.

Queen of Wands

Key Words: Capable, Skill, Intelligence

The Queen of Wands sits regally on her throne, in control of all she surveys. She holds a sunflower and statues of lions decorate the sides of her throne, both symbolic of the power of the Sun and the element of Fire. The lions also bring in the Sun Sign of Leo. These energies bring to this female a balance of masculine and feminine energies.

She is capable of running her own life, as well as directing others toward purposeful achievement. While fair in her situational assessments, the Queen of Wands is capable of planning initiatives and carrying them out. Her yellow crown and gown indicates the element of Air, bringing with it the vibration of mental clarity and intelligence.

The black cat in the forefront provides a spiritual connection to the world as the queen's familiar, a spirit animal that gives messages and provides psychic awareness. The black color of the cat indicates a grounding and protective energy to allow the Queen of Wands to consider the world both mentally and spiritually in a realm of safety. With the wand in hand, it indicates a woman of skill and high capability.

Kings

King of Cups

Key Words: Understanding, Calm, Supportive

The King of Cups denotes a person who has reached the height of emotional understanding. Nothing flutters him. He is cool, calm, and collected in the face of adversity. When consulted on any matter, he can be supportive while remaining emotionally detached.

His patient demeanor is a result of his belief that everything comes in its own time. The King of Cups is able to see the general picture and can impart an overview that brings things into perspective.

This card may also come up when someone is acting hastily or trying to force something to happen. The King of Cups sends the message not to be premature and to handle the situation in a way that takes all aspects into account.

King of Pentacles

Key Words: Wealth, Generosity, Spiritual Advancement

The King of Pentacles represents someone who is wealthy, coming from old money, or having a "rich" family name, such as Dupont or Kennedy. This is most likely a generous person who works in business or industry; could be in finance or banking. In the reverse, this person would present himself as successful, yet in reality is quite the opposite.

This person is one who has not only attained success on the earthly plane in the way of monetary rewards, but who has advanced on the spiritual plane; balancing both and not letting one aspect obscure the other. Success comes from manifesting the spiritual into the physical. They have a following in both worlds. He has the highest values and facilitates the development of others through himself.

King of Swords

Key Words: Decision, Authority, Determination

The King of Swords sits on his throne holding a sword with the blade pointing toward the sky. It is the sword of discrimination, hence the reason this card comes up when there is the need to make a decision. Be careful to look at both sides before making the decision. The King of Swords is a person who looks at things in terms of black and white; there is no gray area. He only wants the facts.

The King of Swords may imply a male in the legal profession, such as a policeman or a lawyer. It could also be an accountant who works for the IRS.

This card also comes up for people who are abusive. It could be an abusive parent or spouse.

The alternative is that the King of Swords represents someone who handles things very well or has the right to authority; the original "buck stops here" person. The male associated with this card is highly masculine in his presentation and mannerisms and could be called macho.

King of Wands

Key Words: Wise, Down-to-earth, Take-charge

The King of Wands (or Rods) sits calmly on his throne, holding a wooden staff; he is dressed in orange robes with green decorating the shoulders and a cape flowing around him. His lion necklace and lion emblems on the banner behind him are imposing compared to the tiny salamander at his feet.

The King of Wands could be a Cancer or Leo. He has a big heart and is the kind of person who sits above the rest and lets people in, but holds them at arm's length. He is a take-charge kind of person, but doesn't have any sense of completion or feels threatened by other people. This King has wisdom to let things just be the way they are and does not interfere. This could also be someone who can allow for the occurrence of simultaneous things without overreacting.

The King of Wands also represents a person who is a good administrator. This person has an earthy side and is very intelligent. He is a people person and spends a lot of time interacting with people. This could mean socially or as a result of his occupation (counselor, social worker, etc.)

9 Ethical Considerations for Psychics

To perform readings in an ethical and responsible way, psychics generally follow these guidelines:

Whatever information is gleaned from the reading, the psychic must always remember not to judge it, or try to put context around it. The information is meant for the subject alone; it does not have to make sense to the reader. It is important to merely say what comes to mind, without attempting to understand the meaning of it. If the information is accurate, the subject will fully understand the impact of the message being conveyed.

All readings should be prefaced with asking that the information be received for the client's highest good and the highest good of those around her. Appropriate intent is required to protect the inquirer's energy from inadvertently being affected by the reader. Properly focused, the reading can create a positive energy shift in the client, thereby opening her to a higher level of understanding.

To use the Tarot as a divining method should be done with caution, as free will is more of a determining factor than pre-destiny. The reading is accurate given the current state of affairs. It is possible for the subject to change her path to avoid a loss or other unpleasant situation and to increase the ability to attain goals. The tarot's value comes in its ability to warn of potential disruption or to allow one to see the situation from a fresh perspective. It is up to the individual to choose what she does with the information.

As a reader, do not intervene or suggest a course of action. It is not for you to decide. Your role is to present the message or information as it comes through you. You are the conduit. Do not insert yourself into another person's path. Do not attempt to exert control.

Some practitioners, and even some clients, are capable of influencing the cards. That is, they are able to influence which cards are drawn or the message that is presented. In the case of the reader, it is especially critical to remain objective and focused on the client's highest good.

The psychic mirrors what is present around the subject. At times, the revelations are disturbing and not what the subject was hoping to hear. The psychic must learn to read the meanings of the cards, as well as to read the ability of the subject to handle the information. Responsible tarot reading is essential for the practitioner.

When delivering bad news, remember that challenges are placed before us to assist in our development. The information can be presented in a way that is inspirational. Try to interject a feeling of hopefulness and growth as a result of whatever negative situation is pending or occurring.

10 Choosing a Practitioner

You've made the decision to seek assistance in your quest and are prepared to invest the time and money to succeed in reaching your goals. The fees vary from one practitioner to the next, but that alone is insufficient to help you make a decision when it comes to selecting a practitioner that aligns with your style, energy level, and desired results. Today, there are more metaphysical practitioners, tarot readers, and spiritual counselors than ever before. All say that they have the ability to improve your life, get you on the right path, and help you reach your goals.

If you are looking for a way to understand your situation from an intuitive perspective, seeking to confirm what you're already feeling, or wanting to generate alternatives, tarot may be a good way to tap into new perspectives on yourself, others, or your situation.

Note: Tarot is inappropriate for use as a decision-making tool or to predict the future. Free will is an essential component when using this modality.

If you're interested in having your cards read, here are some things you should be aware of.

A Tarot reading is an energy exchange, a mingling of energies between you and the reader. Whenever you get a reading, you are giving permission to the psychic to mingle her energies with yours. Before getting a reading, consider how you feel in the presence of the reader. If you experience any discomfort whatsoever, do not proceed with the reading. If you are uncomfortable with the reader's energy, a reading with this person may cause a disruption in your energy field. Allow a reading only if her energy feels good to you. If you get a bad feeling from the reader, do not allow the reading to be performed.

If the reader claims that you have a curse, dark cloud, or negative being attached to you and wants a hefty price to remove it, end the session and leave. A reader who presents you with such expensive strategies is looking for additional income and is not advising you in your best interest.

The reader may ask questions in order to clarify what is coming through. Be as general as possible when providing the information. Avoid details to see how much of the situation is revealed by the cards. Allow important aspects of the situation to surface by themselves.

Tarot will help you to open to a different perspective and to gain understanding about your life and your future. Whatever is revealed to you is just the potential of what could be. If a warning comes through, take heed of what is said. Most warnings are put in place as a safeguard to help avoid a disruptive or disturbing circumstance. You have the power to avert disaster by making appropriate choices.

Whatever topic you ask about, the message may or may not answer your question directly. Whatever message is meant to come through will, regardless of what you think the focus should be. The same message will surface repeatedly if it is something essential in your path. It must be addressed.

Do not act or make any major decisions based solely on the information provided by the psychic. The decision must be made because you feel, beyond a reasonable doubt, that this is what is best for you. Ask yourself if you would have done it the same way, even without the benefit of a reading.

There are times when what is revealed during a reading is shocking due to the private nature of the information. It could be something you thought no one knew. During this type of reading, pay close attention to how you're feeling emotionally. By doing so, a new level of realization may be achieved.

Getting a reading while under the influence of drugs or alcohol is a waste of money. By depressing the central nervous system, the auric field clouds over, making it difficult to read. Under optimal conditions (explained in the section called "Influencing Factors"), you can increase the amount of information that can be ascertained about you.

It is important for you to feel that the reader provides information to you in a caring manner that is for your highest good. Harsh delivery of sensitive information can be detrimental to your state of mind. It is best to come away from the reading with a sense of hope, understanding, and clarity.

10 The Psychology of Tarot

The tarot can serve as a powerful insight tool. In this context, it is a source of objective representations of universal concepts that surface during the course of a human life. Themes throughout many different tarot decks represent psychological aspects of the self. This allows patterns of behaviors, thoughts, and feelings to be revealed during the reading, making it possible to uncover the true nature of the inquirer. By identifying underlying issues or aspects of the self, it is possible for the inquirer to recognize that which is the essence of her core self. This level of identity is the unwavering true self, detached from titles and roles. It is the fundamental nature of the individual. The individual skill level of the reader plays an important role in the depth of information that can be revealed in this manner.

Psychiatrist and personality theorist Carl Jung viewed the tarot as a gateway to the subconscious. His concept of the Archetypes, which are universally recognized, genetically imprinted and instinctual thought patterns passed down through generations, has been reflected in a variety of tarot decks. He viewed the mystical side of life as necessary to self-development and self-actualization.*

In times of crisis, the tarot can serve as an intervention, as it has the ability to console and reassure. The Tarot can be used as a way to generate alternatives in a situation or to provide a new perspective. It allows emotionality to be minimized as it pertains to decisions regarding the issue at hand. At times, the reading assists in creating an energy shift, allowing the inquirer to release pent-up emotions. The subject may cry or become angry during the reading. Afterward, the situation or issue can be seen much more clearly.

Tarot opens the way to identifying blocks to progress, factors that may be preventing the subject from moving forward or beyond a situation or set of beliefs. Refusal to address an issue can be noted and revisited later when the inquirer may have progressed far enough to be able to consider its value. It is essential that the inquirer feels that the message is valid and pertinent to his process. What is revealed depends upon the inquirer's willingness to expose that part of him or herself that has been shrouded in shadow.

Because the focus is on the cards rather than the inquirer, sensitive issues can be freely discussed. The deck serves as the object of the problem, allowing the subject to open to the message and consider the information, without feeling defensive. By stepping back from the issue, the inquirer is able to see the situation without attachment and without resistance. The reader, in this case, serves as the conduit by which the inquirer is able to address the situation more objectively.

Many times, the reading is a confirmation of what the subject already knows or feels to be true. In this case, the tarot serves not as an oracle, but as a mechanism by which the inquirer can feel confident in his or her decision or understanding of a situation.

* For further reading on this topic, try *Discovering Your Self Through the Tarot: A Jungian Guide to Archetypes & Personality* by Rose Gwain and *Tarot As a Way of Life: A Jungian Approach to the Tarot* by Karen Hamaker-Zondag.

Epilogue

The true nature of tarot is that it has the ability to reveal our own true nature. It can assist us on the path to spiritual and psychological growth, if the information is used wisely. Tarot is the tool that allows us to step away from ourselves and gaze upon our lives more objectively. Situations are revealed, and the message can be received without the drama that surrounds it. A reading can uncover possibilities and alternatives as long as the inquirer is open to the messages.

Part psychic, part psychological, the tarot allows our character to unfold before us. The encounter is a spiritual energy exchange, charged with unlimited potentiality. The tarot reveals messages at the proper time; that is, when the inquirer is ready to hear them. If a message is unveiled prematurely, the person will not understand its meaning. Similarly, a person will seek a reading at a time when she is ready to open and recognize the patterns that create the future.

The mystical side of tarot is its deep symbolic and metaphysical roots. The practical side is its ability to be used as a tool to generate alternatives. That is the balanced nature of the tarot. Both mysterious and useful, the tarot draws all types of people into its spell, especially those seeking to understand their lives. They seek to confirm that which the higher Self already knows to be true. What is revealed is that which lies deep within the inquirer. How much is revealed depends upon the openness of the inquirer.

The psychic must use her ability for the highest good of the inquirer; her role is to produce growth and foster understanding. The information that comes through is delivered with goodwill and the intent to help not harm.

There is a responsibility associated with performing a reading. The psychic should not interfere in the path of the inquirer. The information is provided to the client; the inquirer decides how to use it. The ability to move energy must be used with respect and never done without permission from the inquirer. The inquirer should be choosey about who she gives permission to. If the inquirer experiences discomfort in the energy field of the psychic, a reading should not be allowed.

Tarot is designed to enlighten, entertain, perplex, and reveal. The cards are used as an external tool to delve into the depths of the core self. It offers an opportunity to get information about the energy of a situation and suggests ways to transform it into what you want your life to look like. Tarot is a wonderful way to identify the blocks in your path. As you seek to understand and grow, you elevate your vibrational level, as well as the vibration of the whole planet.

As you read my book, we were exchanging energy. It was written with positive intent for the highest good of the readers. I'd like to close with my wishes for you. These wishes can be used as a daily affirmation to invite a positive vibration into your life.

May your path be filled with love and acceptance.
May positive energy follow you on your journey.
May your life be filled with wonder.
May you learn and grow all the days of your life.
May you find peace and joy within your Self.

With many blessings,

Diane Wing

Appendix: A Sample Reading

To provide an understanding about cultivating a flow in the way the cards are read, this sample reading was developed using the five-card *Main Issue* spread.

Let's say the question is asked as, "Give me a message about my current work project."

The cards selected are:

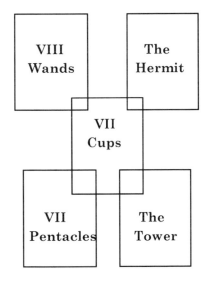

Sample Reading

Starting with the center card, which represents the main issue surrounding the project, we see that there is great potential for success in terms of financial rewards, recognition, and learning from completing the project.

Starting at the top left-hand corner, connected to the VII of Cups is the VIII of Wands. There was much energy put into this project, some of which was fraught with tension.

At the bottom left-hand corner is the VII of Pentacles, indicating that the project had some components that pulled at the creator's past knowledge set and abilities.

The Hermit stands at the right-hand top of the spread, indicating that this person prefers to work alone and create products that light the way for others. This particular project will be in keeping with that and pulls the person's wisdom into a complete package.

The Tower at the bottom right-hand corner shows that caution is needed in the way the person proceeds with the project's launch or may be suggesting that doing things the old way, like going through a certain process to get the project into the right hands, will not work. There is the potential for chaos to erupt if the project launch is not well thought out. As this card is at the end of the spread, its position can be interpreted as an occurrence taking place after all other activities are concluded.

Ultimately, this hand shows that the person who authored the project put themselves into it and did all he could to make it the best possible product. It is only at the hand-off when there is potential for failure.

About the Author

Diane Wing has been in the business of guiding people to reach their full potential for over two decades. She is an intuitive tarot reader, Reiki master, and a lifetime student of metaphysics, mysticism, and spirituality. With a Master's degree in psychology, Diane uses the tarot as a tool to perform insightful readings intended to produce growth and harmony in the lives of her clients.

She is the founder of Wing Academy of Unfoldment, a virtual Mystery school with courses that provide students with convenient and affordable opportunities to expand their understanding of the esoteric arts, metaphysics, and occult sciences. Courses provide a transformative experience, a spiritual unfoldment, where an evolution will take place, with the individual revealing his or her true nature and developing a deeper self-awareness and closer relationship with The Universal Energy. The information is presented via private lessons conducted in person or by phone, self-study, and group teleseminars.

Diane is dedicated to the practical application of metaphysical concepts to help her clients understand and trust themselves, make better decisions, and be more resilient in the face of change. She inspires and transforms others to feel their best and work to fulfill their potential as they strive toward self-mastery. Diane helps them to realize their greatness and to come to terms with their truth, remove delusion, and clear away misconceptions of the self to reveal their true nature at a core level.

She and her husband live in Southeastern Pennsylvania. Diane can be contacted via her websites at **www.ForestWitch.com** and **www.VibrantConcepts.com.**

Bibliography

Gawain, S., & King, L. (1986). *Living in the light*. Mill Valley, CA: Whatever Pub.

Gwain, R. (1994). In *Discovering your self through the tarot: A Jungian guide to archetypes & personality*. Rochester, Vt: Destiny Books.

Greer, J. M. (2003). *The new encyclopedia of the occult*. St. Paul, MN: Llewellyn Publications.

Hamaker-Zondag, K. (1997). In *Tarot as a way of life: A Jungian approach to the tarot*. York Beach, Me: Samuel Weiser.

Hulse, D. A. (2000). *The western mysteries: An encyclopedic guide to the sacred languages & magickal systems of the world: the key of it all,* bk. II. The key of it all, bk. II. St. Paul, Minn: Llewellyn.

Melville, F. (2002). *The secrets of high magic*. Hauppauge, NY: Barron's Educational Series.

Nema. (2003). *The way of mystery: Magick, mysticism & self-transcendence*. St. Paul, Minn: Llewellyn Publications.

The Jerusalem Bible: Reader's edition. (1968). Garden City, N.Y.: Doubleday.

Tresidder, J. (2000). *Symbols and their meanings*. [London]: Friedman/Fairfax.

Wing, D. L. (2003). *The nature of tarot*. Victoria, B.C: Trafford.

Index

"Dimensional Ascension has removed many of the blockages that slow down my work as a Light Worker."
-- Paige Lovitt, *Reader Views* (March 2006)

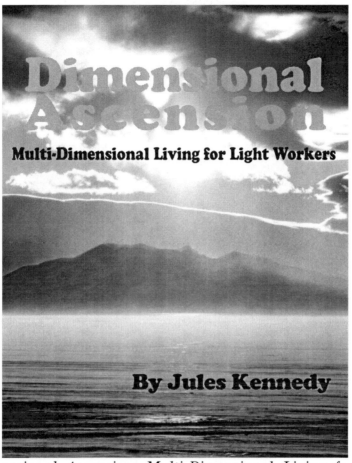

Dimensional Ascension: Multi-Dimensional Living for Light Workers delivers a powerful message that will help anyone speculating the deeper meaning of life here upon this planet.

"What is my purpose?" "Why am I here on earth at this time?" "Will I ever be happy?" These are questions that many people today are asking themselves. This innovative book can help you answer some of the most pressing, intimate concerns in your life. Through Dimensional Ascension learn to tap into the power of your own mind, use imagination to create reality, and access the full capacity of love to transform every relationship in your life.

ISBN 978-1-932690-21-7 • $19.95

Learn More at www.DimensionalAscension.com

"With Awakening Consciousness: A Girl's Guide workbook, children will have a wonderful time exploring their spiritual side. In fact, I believe adults would enjoy it too!"

Kelly Wallace, professional psychic counselor
author *10 Minutes A Day to a Powerful New Life!*

Awakening Consciousness is a workbook designed to encourage spiritual growth on a path of self awareness. The fun hands-on exercises in this motivating, easy to use workbook are for girls of all ages and will encourage great exploration into universal awareness.

- Exercise your seven chakras
- Learn about crystals
- Discover how to keep a healthy aura
- Explore your inner self
- Practice learning the pendulum
- Create your own future
- Try aromatherapy with easy to do, fun crafts

ISBN 978-1-932690-80-4 • $16.95

Learn more at www.AwakeningGirls.com

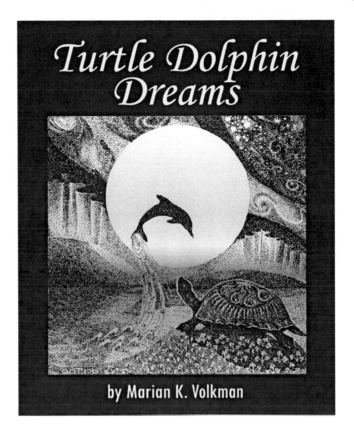